WORK YOURSELF OUT OF A JOB

Take Control of Your Destiny and Reap the Rewards You Desire

DALE TYSON

ISBN: 1500891894
ISBN 13: 9781500891893

Contents

Foreword

Work Yourself Out of a Job by Dale Tyson is to inform you of an alternative to being stuck in a lousy job you hate because of not being paid what you are worth, boss and coworkers are a jerk, being harassed, not appreciated, and other reasons.

Your alternative is to start a business. It is normal to not know what you what to do and you may have concerns because you do not know what to do.

This book provides information, suggestions, stories, tips, and more to help you create your journey from employee to business owner. Dale provides a comprehensive and structured DPIE Model ™ process and discussion of supporting documents for you to use.

His book is based on over 30 years of business ownership and corporate world knowledge, skills and experiences.

Learn from Dale how you can Work Yourself Out of a Job – to Take Control of Your Destiny and Reap the Rewards You Desire.

Raymond Aaron
Author - **Branding Small Business for Dummies**
NY Times Bestselling Author

Preface

The intent of this book is to provide information to help people create a journey from being an employee, or unemployed, to being a small business owner. This information can also help people who already have a small business that is struggling and wants information and ideas for improvements. Our Mission is "Providing information and assistance to new or existing business owners so they can reap the rewards they desire".

The information is intended for a small business with 1 or 2 people, or up to about 20 - 30 people. This can also be used if you want a "hobby" or part time business.

The difference is what needs to be done, how comprehensive some of the plans are, the types of documents, and the amount of effort to start it. A 1 or 2 person business could be operating in several months with a few combined plans and some documents being several pages. A 20 – 30 person business will take longer to start, will have more dedicated plans and related documents for various aspects of the startup.

This information is applicable for people who have no, or a limited, or a lot of business knowledge. The difference is how fast and easily they move through the startup process. The complexity of the business will also be a factor. Everyone will arrive at their destination.

Do not "over think" or "panic" about what you need to do. It is normal to have concerns and apprehension when doing something new. Reading this book and following the process will control these. Having a little apprehension is a good way to keep you thinking and learning.

This book is based on knowledge, skills and experiences from starting and operating several of my own businesses, and talking with other owners. This also includes my knowledge, skills, and experiences having various types of jobs in many industries.

I started my entrepreneur activities when I was about 6 years old selling lemonade, then about 9 years old mowing yards and shoveling snow, and a paper route. I also rode my bike around picking up and returning glass soda bottles for the deposit. Yes, this was numerous years ago.

I was 20 years old and dissatisfied going to university so I started my first full time business owning and driving a taxi. I leveraged my car to maximize my revenue by leasing it to other drivers when I was not driving. Owning and operating the taxi paid all my bills and had money to play with. This was part of a franchise so it was very easy to start. After a year I was bored and someone offered me a job I liked, so I sold the car.

Just after getting married I started a part time home maintenance business doing a variety of handyman jobs for extra money. I did this for many years until the kids were born.

Years later I wanted to start a full time business, but a few of us bought an Executive Suite and Secretarial Service business. My wife managed it full time with an employee. I have certain work responsibilities. After 13 years, we sold it and it still exists today.

As the kids left home and with my job uncertainty when another company bought the company I was working for, I decided to start a couple real estate related businesses. The knowledge, skills, and experiences from my home maintenance business are a great advantage to my current real estate businesses. This was a Plan B in case I was laid off or got to the point I could leave my job. I Worked Myself Out of a Job.

I have a couple real estate businesses, but they do not require my full time attention. I have other people and companies performing the majority of the activities.

I listened to a NY Best Selling author talk about writing a book about your expertise to help other people. I had my "light bulb" moment to use my business ownership knowledge, skills, and experiences and combine with my corporate world Business Planning, Business Analyst, and Project Management knowledge, skills, and experience to create a comprehensive and structured process with the supporting documents to help other people start their journey to business owner.

As a Project Manager, you have an objective, you determine what needs to be done, create plans to guide you, perform the activities, track the results, make adjustments as needed, and complete the objective.

Starting a business is the same. You investigate and decide what you are going to do, what needs to be done, how are you going to accomplish the activities, and take action. This is not "rocket science".

This is where the book comes in. It involves my DPIE Model™ process with information, supporting documents, templates, and examples for you use.

The model represents the Discovery, Planning, Implementation, and Expansion elements to start a business. The process involves a variety of information and supporting documents such as a Lesson Plan, Business Information document, Master Plan, and a few others. We can also provide various types of assistance to help you create a guide for your journey to business owner.

As in life, there are things that I did well, things that I would do different, and things that I would not do again. The old sayings of "hind sight is 20/20" and "learn from other people's mistakes" still apply.

I did not have any formal process when starting my prior businesses, but I took the time and effort to learn what I needed to do, create a plan of activities, and performed the work to complete the journey.

We want to help people get out of their unrewarding jobs and start their own business. I hope with the information provided in this book and the information available, many people will be able start and be successful in their business.

If you are looking for or thinking about a "Get Rich" scheme, that reading an article with "The 7 Secrets to Start a Business" will provide the structure and information you need, and that it does not require any time, effort or money, then STOP READING THIS BOOK!

If you are willing to follow a comprehensive and structured process and take action to change your life, then CONTINUE READING THIS BOOK!

You realize great results are the result of some time, effort, research and resources, therefore continue reading. Yes, people can occasionally succeed without using a process, but you want to have a tremendous advantage by having and following a process. You need to take control of your own destiny and not leave it to luck or some scheme.

For those of you currently employed, our recommendation is for you to continue with your salary, benefits, and some amount of security with your job. Use our process, information and assistance to create the business you want to own to the point where you can transition from your present job to owning your business.

Going through the entire process and doing all the work will greatly improve your chances for success. This will lead to the freedom and rewards you want. This will also work if you are unemployed, but you will need to accelerate the schedule, scale back what you start with, and expand a little differently.

The book's title of **Work Yourself Out of a Job** is just that. I had a couple businesses while I had a job. Starting a real business will take time, effort, and resources, and will take perseverance, patience, and faith. The sub title is Take Control of Your Destiny and Reap Your Rewards. The rewards can go beyond money to doing what you want or love, having more control of your life, and helping others.

Some people may criticize this book because this is not professionally written and it relates to a business. It is not a novel or fiction, and is not based on researching other books and information online. The one thing about books, they do not mean anything until you extract information to apply it by taking action.

The combination of this book and all the business resources is intended to provide you a roadmap to start and complete your journey.

For some people, this book is a reminder of what to do and they can start their journey now. I wish them all the success they desire. Most people will need additional information and assistance.

You can go to the company website for the more contact and journey information at www.LYLBusinessDevelopment.com or send us an email to start@LYLBusinessDevelopment.com.

Introduction

It is impossible for any single book to include all the details for every aspect of starting and operating a business. The objective of this book is to omit the typical "fluff" found in most "how to" books and provide enough information for you to learn what needs to be done to start your business and what are your next steps on your journey.

It includes stories, tips, and a page at the end of the chapters to write Ideas, Questions, and Actions. Understanding and taking action are very important to your success in every aspect of your life, including starting a business.

Depending on your business, some activities will not apply and some activities you will learn to add. Every business is like a fingerprint, there are common and unique characteristics.

The primary purpose of every business is to serve their current and prospective customers. This is done by providing products, services, and information. The rewards are the result of adding value that your customers are willing to pay you for.

This book goes into the core business functions and aspects of starting and operating a small business. The functions have been in place for thousands of years in various ways. The functions include Finance, Accounting, Marketing, Operations, and others. There are detailed activities you need to do within each function such as doing bookkeeping in Accounting, running an advertisement in Marketing, and assembling products or have information in Operations. Your business will have similarities and differences within each of the functions compared to other businesses – even in the same industry.

Let's take a look at finance as one core business function. Every business needs money to start and operate. The questions include how much is needed and when, how is it raised, and do you need to repay it and when. There are many resources for money from personal, friends and family (with extra care), loans, and partners. The financial package is one part of your journey to being a business owner.

There are agencies and organizations with information about the percentage of businesses failures in the 1st through 5th year. There are reasons like they ran out of money, bad location, got "burned out", and others.

If you dig deeper, I would estimate that 80% of the failures are **really** because the owner did not have and use a comprehensive process, and did not create and follow the appropriate plans. If they ran out of money, it is probably because they spent it on the wrong things, took too much out for personal items, not save enough for growth or contingencies, and did not have financial controls and reporting to identify and correct problems before they became really big.

There are natural concerns and apprehension of starting a business. So how do you overcome these and dramatically increasing your odds of success — use a comprehensive and structured process that goes through a Discovery and a Planning phase before you Implement the startup, and be working on your Expansion all the time.

The DPIE Model ™ is a basic and logical process. The process involves various required, recommended, and optional documents associated with starting a business. Which ones you use will depend on the type and size of your business. One of the core process documents is a Lesson Plan with Questions and Actions (Lesson Plan) which is part of the Discovery element. The book will reference several other documents relating to the process.

As you follow the process to start the business, each of the aspects will eventually be broken down into activities that are common with other businesses and unique to your business. Therefore, in the pre-populated support documents, there will be some activities that will be changed, some will not apply, and some you will need to add. The support documents will become customized to your business.

For example, if your business is renting space in a building you will need leasing activities, so you do not need the buying activities. Some of the human resources activities will not apply if you are the sole person with a Limited Liability Company and classified as a disregarded entity. We'll provide more information throughout the book.

Robert Kiyosaki talks about an income quadrant with the left side top as **Employee**, left side lower as **Self Employed**, right top as **Business Owner**, and right lower as **Investor**. I'm using the phrase "business owner" throughout our information to mean either Self Employed or Business Owner.

Being an Employee is not what this book is about. It is about building a business so you can get out of your lousy job. Getting to be an Investor may be the ultimate goal of being a business owner.

You need to have "intentional congruency" within your business, and when you have more than one business. The intentional means deliberately having and following a strategy and plans with objectives. The congruency is about working together to increase efficiencies whether it involves objects or activities. For example using the same equipment to build two different products can increase revenue and save money. The landlord and flipping businesses can use the same trades people. These are different entities for various reasons, but they share resources.

The "intentional congruency" may be part of your expansion. You need to get the business started quickly with 1 or 2 core products and/or services and add more later. You can create or buy another business later if it fits your vision.

This book is all about creating a roadmap from Employee to Self Employed or Business Owner. Your business can be part-time or full time.

I like Alan Lakein's quote that fits with this book and starting your business - **"Time = Life, Therefore, waste your time and waste your life, or master your time and master your life."** Take this a step further by using your time doing what you want to do and reaping your rewards.

Setting Up Your Business

I want to insert a comment about the use of this book before you start reading it. The comment belongs in the Introduction, but many people do not read the Preface and Introduction – they want to jump into the book. I was guilty of doing this.

Therefore, this book is not to sit on a shelf in mint condition. It is intended to be a workbook with highlighting, underlining, putting asterisks (*) by sentences, and what I love – blank pages to write Ideas, Questions, and Actions. You should need more space to write these so get some extra paper or notepad for now. There is a Business Information document you will use to enter all the information you gather. More about this later.

Keep your job as long as you can so there is time to go through the process to start a business. You have time to think and commit to what you want to do, work on numerous activities, and make adjustments. I assure you that as you go through Discovery and Planning you will be thinking of more activities to do – carry a small notepad in your pocket or purse with a pen so you can write down ideas when you think of them.

If you are unemployed or work part time, you will have far more time to accelerate your journey to business owner. You may need to start smaller to save money.

Not Everyone Wants or Can be a Business Owner:

"Every choice moves us closer to or farther away from something. Where are your choices taking your life?" Eric Allenbaugh (Author and Lecturer)

Some people have no interest or desire to own and operate a business and this is fine for people who absolutely love their job. It fulfills their financial, physical, and emotional needs. There are people who have won a lottery or been given a life changing amount of money, but they keep their job. I wish them a very fulfilling life.

However, you may be like most people who are not happy or hate your job and want to get out. Almost anyone can start and operate a business if they have a strong desire to get out of their lousy job, have big reasons "why" to persevere through obstacles to succeed, have the mental ability to learn and do, are willing to work smart, know it takes time and resources, and realize they will need help from others.

Everyone is different and there is no mold for a business owner. There is no defined set of key attributes for a successful business owner. There are successful business owners who are grumpy or friendly, aggressive or patient, proactive or reactive, willing or not willing to learn from others, and have or do not have a strategy.

Let's be honest, some business people are jerks, cheat, and provide bad service and yet make lots of money. I hope you are the opposite and work well with others, provide valuable products and services, and receive the money and other rewards you desire.

There are many people with the "shiny penny syndrome" which means something catches their attention, so they go after it, and then realize it does not interest them or it does not provide what they want. Be careful who you listen to and be far more careful when someone says how easy it is to do their business, that you do not need any money, or other marketing clichés.

Just because everyone cannot be an owner, does NOT mean that you need to remain working for someone else. You are reading this book and there is a process you can follow for your journey to business owner.

Story:

My parents encouraged us to get good grades in school so we could get a good job. Many decades ago, the majority of people would work for 1 or 2 companies and retire with a good pension and social security.

Fast forward several decades and much of this have changed. The average person will have 5 or 6 jobs during their career, many private companies have discontinued pensions because it is a financial liability, and some companies have been so badly mismanaged that they go bankrupt – remember Enron and World Com. Who knows what is going to happen with social security.

If you become unemployed, depending on your age, work experience, and salary, it can be difficult or almost impossible to find another comparable job. I met someone with a graduate degree who was laid off and now works part time at an equipment rental company. He is building a business to do consulting and tutoring.

I worked for Compaq Computer in Houston headquarters and it was bought by Hewlett-Packard (HP) Computer. Obviously there were confidential meetings to decide what would happen to the employees and facilities of both companies. Therefore, there were all sorts of rumors.

I needed a Plan B to look for a new job or start a business just in case I was asked to leave. My choice was start a business. For several reasons, it was easy for me to pick real estate. The question was what type of real estate business.

When you research real estate businesses, there are numerous different types. It is like saying you are a doctor. This is a very general term. The doctor could be a general practitioner, podiatrist working on feet or a brain surgeon, and numerous other types between these.

One real estate business was to buy and rent houses to have monthly cash flow and build equity (assets). Decades before working at Compaq, I bought audios (cassettes back then) and books on "How to buy real estate with no down payment" and other titles. They sat on the shelf gathering dust.

There were many Realtors I worked while doing the home maintenance part time business. Some of them owned rentals, so I signed up to get my real estate license to become a Realtor and learn about investing. About a week into the classes, I realized you do not learn anything about investing. However, I still had the intent to be a Realtor to have access to information that other investors did not have, to have multiple streams of income because the real estate market is always changing which affects income, and to understand the thinking of Realtors and how to communicate with them.

At the same time I was getting my licensee, I found several ways to learn about various types of real estate investing. I joined several organizations, attending numerous networking meetings, free and paid classes, and took action. I bought my first rental property a couple months after getting my license and a second property several months later.

Do you want out of your job for various reasons and want to have control of your own destiny by owning a business? I left HP and do a few types of real estate businesses.

The majority of real estate business is done by other people, so I had time to write this book and all the associated documents, and be able to help people do what I did – create a journey to business owner.

Tip:

Understand your strengths, weaknesses, and what can help and hurt you. There are many methods and processes to help you understand your strengths and what you need to improve. This applies to your personal life and to your business. You need to work to improve both personal and business aspects because a crappy life will affect your business and vice versus.

These methods are a bit more advance, but you can apply the concept in a simpler manner by just writing them down (honestly) and going to our website "Resource" page for a very good book about Personalities types and how to understand yourself and others.

One method I have used in my jobs and business is called SWOT – Strengths, Weaknesses, Opportunities, and Threats. It creates a four quadrant matrix. This can be used for your job and personal objectives.

SWOT Matrix

Strength		
Weakness		

Threat   Opportunity

The Strengths are what you are good or great at doing, but some of these you may not do. You will have roles and responsibilities in your business and what you are good at may not be worth your time or you have higher priority activities.

The Weaknesses include what you do not know and what you struggle with. These should be done by someone else, or you become more knowledgeable. Becoming knowledge does not mean you are going to do them, but you need to understand how they fit your business objectives. To be successful, find other people to do these.

You may say you like to mow the grass. The total time to change clothes, get the equipment out, do the mowing and edging, cleaning and putting the equipment away, and you getting cleaned up could take a few hours. Your time as an owner should be worth at least $50 per hour so you have consumed $150 of your time – which can be more valuable than money. So hire someone for $50 to do the yard. You can use this time to do more activities on your journey or apply to your relax time. Okay – if doing the yard work is truly relaxing, then do it as part of your relax time.

The Opportunities involve situations that can help you and your business. These include creating a new product, finding a major customer, and expanding your business. By identifying these you can include them in a plan to do now or in the future.

The Threats involve situations that can hurt you and your business. These include staff and suppliers not performing, not tracking the work you outsource, not following up with people, and more efficient technology you do not have. There is a way to reduce or eliminate these.

A second method involves personality profiles. There is documented use of profiles going back 2,500 years ago to the Greek physician Hippocrates.

A common name for the four profiles is DISC. This is a four quadrant matrix. The "D" is for Dominance, the "I" is for Influence, the "S" is for Steadiness, and the "C" is for Conscientious.

DISC Matrix

	Task	People
Extravert	Dominance	Influence
Introvert	Conscientious	Steadiness

Everyone has some amount of all four styles, but there is one that is your primary style or you are on the border of two styles. Some people will use "high" or "low" for their style to indicate a level. How you determine your style is to measure the level (degree) of how Introverted or Extraverted you are and how Task or People oriented you are.

Understanding the traits of the profiles will let you understand how you think and act, and how people in your family, friends, and business life think and act. You can learn to communicate better with them.

For an example, a consultant "I" is helping a manager "C" resolve a problem. The consultant wants to talk a lot and have fun, and the manger just wants to know the facts to find and fix the problem. The consultant needs to tone down his personality and provide the information.

Your Reasons to be a Business Owner:

"I'd asked around 10 or 15 people for suggestions. Finally one lady friend asked the right question, 'Well, what do you love most?' That's how I started painting money." Andy Warhol (Artist and Business person)

The WHY is one of the most important questions to answer before starting a business. Like your job, you will spend hours involved with it. Starting and operating a business is a form of work, but you have more control of your life.

Why do you want to leave your job?
- Being harassed in different ways?
- Boss is an idiot, micro managing, and steal your ideas?
- Not being paid what you are worth and concrete ceiling? There is no hope or take 5 to 10 years

for 1 more step up the job ladder. Look at how many employees and then how many people are at the level you want to get to.

- People being laid off and you wonder when they will call you?
- Working excessive hours, and probably for no extra money?
- Unrealistic demands?
- Bored doing the same thing?
- Colleagues are jerks and back-stabbing?
- Not having any fun?
- Feel that you would be happier working you yourself?

Here are a few reasons to have a business:
- You want to follow your passion.
- You want to have more control of your life.
- You want the financial and other rewards from your work.
- You want to improve your lifestyle.
- You want control of who you work with.
- You want to decide what to do.
- You want to complete and take pride in your accomplishments.

The "whys" are your key motivators, the reason to get up enthusiastically every day and to persevere even when something is not going right. If you did very good work creating and following the plans from Discovery to Implementation, there will be fewer things go off track and will have less impact on the business and you.

Everyone has different desires that motivate them. The most common is financial, but there is a physical and emotional element. Some are self-centered, but the focus needs to be on helping others. Which combinations make you want to do something different – to get out of your job? You'll understand that doing something only for the purpose of making money usually does not work. You need to provide solutions, value, and service that people are willing to pay for.

The financial aspects include having money, credit, income producing assets like a true investor, and others. Money is an object that represents value. Put a dollar bill on the table and food does not appear, a utility bill does not get paid, and does not get you to a vacation spot. You substitute it for something. If it costs more than the money you have, then we have a bad habit of charging it and pay for it over time. You need to manage your money wisely to get ahead of being broke.

The physical aspects are external. They include objects that you can touch and things that you can do, such as a have a house, car, travel, and many others. Some are free so the financial does not apply such as taking the kids to a park. Some are cheap such as going to a movie. Some are relatively expensive such as a 10 day cruise with a balcony suite.

The emotional aspects are internal. They are about personal satisfaction and pride that you get from accomplishing your journey, a sincere thank-you from a customer, and respect and trust from others.

There is an expectation for us to be loyal to the company and for the company to be loyal to its employees. However, no one from the line workers to the CEO is exempt from losing their job. A company may need to lay off people to survive for the benefit of the remaining employees, suppliers, and customers. How much control do you have in keeping your job?

You have a position ceiling at your job. How long has your manager been in the position? How many others in your department are qualified (or not) to take over when they leave? Or worst, they bring in someone else from outside the company. Do you want to wait for something to happen before you to get promoted, if it ever happens? You need to have more control of your work and life.

A major reason why people do not want to start a business is the unknown. There can be concerns, apprehension, or fear. These are and will always be part of human nature. Each person has a different set of them and to varying degrees, from it has very little effect occasionally to paralyzing them. These relate to real or perceived situations, and starting a business can be one of them.

There is an acronym about FEAR. This is not to make light of fears that really affect people.

- False
- Evidence
- Appearing
- Real

The biggest way to overcome the unknown of starting a business is to have a comprehensive and structured process to take you a step at a time to identify what to do and find people to help you. As you go through the process you gather information and make progress which removes the unknowns and builds your confidence.

You may a concern, apprehension, or fear of competing with established competitors. As you go through a process, you learn they can directly or indirectly help you and identify what you can do better. There are ways for you to research and interact with them to learn what to do and what not to do. Your negative thoughts subside once you know what makes you special.

A way to overcome a fear of starting a business is to have a far bigger fear of having to endure all the things that you dislike or hate about your job such as being harassed, not earning what you are worth, and other reasons.

Michael Irvin retired from the Dallas Cowboys football team. He won a college championship, 3 football Superbowls, and is in the Hall of Fame. I heard him speak a few times and when asked if he feared getting hit all the time playing football, he said his fear of getting hit was FAR LESS than his fear of going back into poverty. He was motivated and took action to succeed.

Mistakes in business may have very little impact or can be a major setback. This is part of business and life. Having a clear vision, good information and solid plans will remove or minimize the occurrence and the impact. I know a couple who had their car reposed and went bankrupt, but they are now multi-millionaires. One key to success is to learn from past mistakes and issues so you do not repeat them and better yet – learn what to do better. Not learning from a mistake should be a crime.

A few questions to answer honestly:
- Do you want to continue to utilize your skills at a lousy job for the company's benefit, not for you?
- Do you understand there is a comprehensive and structured process to follow?

- Do you understand there is a way to overcome the concerns, apprehension or fear of starting your business?
- Do you understand you will need help from various people?

Story:

Going back to me being about 7 years old selling lemonade allowed me to buy more candy, comic books, and toys. Then I moved up to mowing grass and shoveling snow for more money. Then I had a magazine route for more money.

I started going to university and was not motivated. For a part time job I drove a taxi. When I dropped out of university I started my first full time business when I was 20 years old owning a taxi. After a year I was bored and went to work for a large department store as a department head. With a series of events where I worked and some people saying "get a degree and get a good job", I returned to university and finished my business degree.

I started a new job after graduating. There was limited money so I started a part time home maintenance business. This kept me busier, but the extra money was great. I stopped doing this after the kids were born.

At another job I was "pigeon holed" having a business degree in an engineering business so I started looking for a business to buy – the entrepreneur bug was back. My wife was tired of her job, so we and my parents ended up buying a company that she managed full time with an employee. We owned it for 13 years and increased the sales and profit about 500%. I stayed at my job so my entrepreneur spirit was on hold.

My last journey into full time business ownership was a result of HP buying Compaq. I created and completed a Plan B journey from employee to owner. This story was discussed in a previous section.

Tip:

NEVER stop learning. You spend your life learning unintentionally and intentionally. As you start a business you will learn as a result of the information gathered and experiences.

Once the business is operating, do not get complacent. It is okay to get the business stabilized, but do not get lazy. You will probably want to make more money and have more free time so you need to learn how to increase revenue, learn ways to do things faster, easier, better, and cheaper to reduce expenses and have more time for fun. You may want to expand which will require learning what and how to accomplish the objectives.

There are numerous changes that can cause negative issues with the business and/or you. Sometimes they can be positive. This includes the local and regional economy, other businesses, transportation changes, local and national government regulations, and many others. By continuing to learn what can affect you, you can prepare for them. The negative can be called risk mitigation, emergency preparedness, or having a Plan B. The positive can be an opportunity IF it fits your Vision and you can create a plan to incorporate properly.

A smart person will learn from their mistakes, a wise person learns from other people's mistakes, and a genius applies what they learned.

You can find and learn from mentors and coaches who have experiences in what you are trying to do and the ability to provide guidance. A good coach is not an expense, but an asset in your pending and future business. They add far more value than the cost.

Being a Business Owner:

"Nothing changes if nothing changes." Earnie Larson (Author and Lecturer)

I already mentioned Robert Kiyosaki's 4 types of income in his Rich Dad, Poor Dad and Cashflow Quadrant books. The intent of my book is to get you out of being an **Employee** and into either being **Self Employed** or a **Business Owner**.

A basic difference between being Self Employed and being a Business Owner is how involved you are in running the business and how it affects your income. A Self Employed person is the business and basically gets paid when they work. If a single attorney runs the business they make money, but if they do not or cannot work for a month, they do not make money. If they have a capable person working in the office there may be some income.

A Business Owner has other people do the majority of the work. They may be involved very little or a lot in operating the business. If they are out for a month, the business should continue to operate and create income. How well the business does will depend on the abilities of the other people – maybe the business operates better and makes more profit with less interference from the owner.

The 4th is not part of this book. It is an **Investor** who has enough money and knowledge to use their financial assets to make enough income to support their lifestyle. Here a person may not be involved in any "business" or they are a passive owner and not involved in the regular operations of the business. They could be involved in the strategy and the overall performance. This is where many people want to be.

For this book being Self Employed or a Business Owner has the same objective of not having a job. The journey's process is the same. The difference is what size and scope of business do you want.

If you want to have a part time business to make some extra money and hopefully do something you enjoy, then great. If you want a full time business with just you or a few others and it provides what you want, then great. If you want to build it bigger and are willing to do the additional work (or lack of work with properly trained employees) to provide what you want, then great.

Starting a business is going to take some time, some effort, some sacrifices, some resources, and there will be some distractions. Going from employee to business owner is going to require a change in what you think about, what you do, how you do things, and others. Remember to follow a process, and create and use your plans and documents for a complete roadmap and an easier journey. **This does not** mean it needs to be complex, take a year or more, hundreds of thousands of your money, and become a recluse.

It does not take very long for the majority of employees to find their job is a routine. Moving to a new job, getting promoted, changing companies or a new career will break the routine for a period of time. Your new job can have different types of problems to solve, but still be fairly routine. For example you may troubleshoot and repair bull dozers, but after several years the majority of the work is the same. If you work with several types of equipment, then it can be less routine, but do you want to do this for the next 30 years or more when you have another passion that can be a business?

Starting a business is not routine. There are several factors that will determine if or how routine your business will become. Your abilities and the complexity of the business will determine how long it takes for activities to become routine. You will need to do periodic improvements and expansions which will disrupt the routine for a period of time and provide other benefits. You will have control of how routine your business becomes.

As you discover all the activities to be completed, you will learn many things that you did not know existed. As an example you may not know that certain types of business entities (in the USA) need an IRS SS-4 to get an Employee Identification Number (EIN) and you can either apply online or sometimes the form needs to be completed and sent in.

Everything you do from the very beginning of the journey to being a business owner will take some amount of work. Some of the work you know and some you will find out, some you will find easy and some you will find difficult, some you will do and some will be done by others. There is no magic business owner fairy to wave a wand and the activities are done.

Doing the activities will take time. Some will take a short amount and some will take a lot, some you have control over and some you will not. The best thing to reduce the time is to have a great plan, and prioritize your work on the appropriate activities. I believe and try my best using Alan Lakein's quote **"What is the best use of my time right now?"**

You will probably need to sacrifice some personal and family time in the beginning and during the initial operating. You will have more time freedom as the activities become routine, hire more people, outsource activities, and make process improvements.

Outsourcing is contracting with a person or company as a supplier or service provider to do work for you such as manufacturing part or all of your product, provide accounting services, virtual assistant, and many other business tasks. The actual work is usually done outside your location and may be in or out of your country.

As you go through the discovery and planning elements, you will come across numerous sources of information. Keep a Business Information document with a summary or details of the information you gather and reference the source. Some of the information will become an activity and included in the plans, and some will be part of the content in your information, product and service.

There will be distractions and obstacles to overcome when starting and operating a new business. Some of your activities will not go as planned. As you go through Discovery and Planning, think of things that could go wrong and include alternatives in your plans. Some problems could cause delays, extra costs, and a change in direction. Do not give up easy. Keep persevering. Do more research and talk with experts. Find a solution or another path – not destination. This is when you test your passion and commitment to your vision and mission.

If you want to keep complaining about your job and life and are not willing to do something about it, then stop reading this book. After all, the guys are coming over to drink a bunch of beers and watch the game so all of you can sit around and complain about your lousy jobs. Why not take some time to get your own business operating and afford a luxury box in the stadium drinking beers and complaining that you had to change hotels for the Superbowl, or had to postpone the weeklong fishing trip to Grand Cayman.

Story:

When I started the journey to do real estate, I needed to structure each business with some type of entity to help protect my personal assets, be able to deduct appropriate expenses, and present myself professionally.

I have a business degree so I had an idea of what business entities to use. I spoke with a few people to confirm the type of entity to use.

There is a Limited liability Corporation (LLC) entity in the USA. The IRS has 3 basic ways the LLC entity can be "taxed". This is different than the entity structure. The IRS can tax the LLC business – as a "disregarded entity", a "corporation", or as a "partnership".

There are different ways to set up the entity and the IRS. I did some online research to find a company to set up the first LLC. They charge an amount on top of the state's filing fee. The company I used provided me all the required documents such as Operating Agreement, Banking Resolutions, and others. Now I have a template for the other LLCs I create.

If you have different types of businesses for various reasons, you need to consider putting them in different business entities. The different entities have contradictions in business record keeping, income distribution, short or long term financial strategy, estate planning, and other factors. Each type of entity has pros and cons.

Based on your knowledge of setting up entities and tax classifications, you can use an online company, or you can do yourself if you really know what you are doing, but still check with a couple experts. Regulations and your life's situation change so another entity may be better.

If you have not set up a business in the last year using an expert or have the slightest doubt about what entity and tax classification, then talk with a couple different types of experts in entity structure, taxation, and estate planning to pick the best entity and tax classification.

Tip:

My guess is 90% of people say they do not have time to start a business. Everyone in the world from the poorest to the richest has 24 hours in a day, the question is – how do you spend it?

Here are some ways to allocate up to 20 hours per week to work on your business, even if you are "busy". Some are obvious yet people will not do them because they are not motivated enough to get out of their lousy job.

First, reduce your TV watching or other "entertainment" to a several hours per week, not per day – particularly on the weekends. Use your time for making progress toward reaching your destination.

Use a digital video recorder (DVR) to record shows and watch them at a later time. Consider watching 2 or 3 times a week a couple hours before going to bed or when you are tired and losing focus on your work. The recordings save you about 33% by fast forward through commercials – a one hour show is really about 40 minutes. When you watch 3 shows you save an hour that is used on your business.

Second, get up an hour earlier or go to bed an hour later or a combination. To reduce the shock to your body, make a 15 minute change for that week, and then another 15 minute change the following week, and continue.

Remember, you are creating a new habit and it takes a little time and effort.

Third, use your time during commuting, lunch, waiting for appointments, and other idle time to do some work. What you can work on will depend on where you are and what is available. Many times I bring my laptop or tablet when there are larger idle times, particularly for gathering information and writing content with or without internet access. I almost always bring a slim black notepad holder to write ideas, questions, and actions. You could use a little notepad that fits in your pocket or purse. These are transferred to the appropriate document regularly.

Fourth, change your commute time. When your commute involves heavy traffic and you spend most of the time stopped or going 10 miles per hour so leave much earlier or later so your overall drive time is less. Use the extra time for your business activities.

Fifth, have a book in your car, briefcase or bag to read when you arrive early, waiting for someone to show up, and other idle time. Obliviously, do not read when driving. You can read a book in a month or two. There are books and articles focused on every aspect of a business and autobiography's of successful people.

When you have "life" disruptions at home, book a meeting with yourself at a quiet location in the house or find a library, bookstore, coffee shop, or other place to get activities done. Some have information and/or internet access available.

Let people know you are not available during this time. Do not answer the phone or read and respond to emails unless it directly relates your "prioritized" business activity, do not work on any non-business activities, and stay focused.

A person told me during this time he does not answer the phone for his family unless there is a 2nd call which means some type of emergency. If you have a phone that texts, they could send a text for emergencies.

Your Business:

"Anything worth doing, is worth doing right" Hunter S. Thompson (Journalist and Author). I would like to teak to "Starting a business is worth doing, so do it right".

It is perfectly normal not to know exactly what you want to do at this time. You may know the type of business at this time and as you go through the process you complete the journey, or you find it is not what you expected and find another type of business to pursue. You may be very good at your job, which may or may not have anything to do with your business.

A good place to start is think about what you are currently doing and what you have done in previous jobs, what you are an expert in, and enjoy or passionate about. A simple answer is do what you are doing, but you own the business. This is great for trades (plumbers, electricians, and others), for professionals (attorney, dentist, and others), and for business skills (marketing, accounting, and others).

Although there can be a simple answer to what type of business, there are activities to be done. The time to start these types of businesses is less because of your knowledge, skills, and experiences. How much it costs to start will depend on the type and size of the business. You will have an expansion plan with an estimate of how much more money you need and when.

The business can be just you as Self-employed or create a true Business with a few employees and/or partners to share the work.

You need to have or build some level of expertise. Don't be concerned about what an "expert" is. An expert is simply a person more knowledgeable that other people – no one knows everything – despite what some people think! To a 1st grader, a 6th grader is a genius, and the same 6th grader is a peon to a 10th grader.

The critical question is - can you provide information, products, services, answer questions and add value to your targeted customers? If so, you are an expert to them. Don't worry about the others who think you are a peon. Remember, you will always be learning so you will increase your expertise to help more people.

There may be entry barriers that make it more challenging to start the business. The barriers can be the high startup cost, complex technology, patents, and lack of experience. You will be in a strong position if you can pass through or around the barriers. Otherwise it may not be possible for you to start, or it will take more time, effort, and resources that you are willing and able to do.

If you want to start a business that is different from your previous job experiences ask "what am I passionate about"? What are my hobbies, sports, fitness or other activities that could be marketable? There are ways to determine if your idea is marketable.

Your best business could be a franchise. There are great ones and there are scams so research is needed. The ones done right have created everything you need to know and do to get started and operate. These will provide training and support to get you started and keeps you going. This can be the easiest and fastest way to get your own business. They can be relatively expensive, but you could be operating in months which save a huge amount of time and effort. There is probably a franchise for any type of business you are interested in.

Franchises should have requirements to join such as your financial situation (cash, net worth, credit score), commitment to adhere to the company procedures, and maybe personal references. Look around and beyond where you live for ideas. You can find franchise opportunities by searching online, go to a grocery or book store to find magazines, or contact a franchise broker.

Reminder to be very cautious about a franchise because there are a bunch that have great marketing, great projections, great stories, but are not viable businesses or maybe a scam. Continue going through this book to learn how to start a business and apply to what they are offering.

Your business could be already started and operating, and you don't know it yet. It is unlikely you will find a "For Sale" sign in the window. The majority of times the owner does not want the employees or other people to know they want to sell.

There are many business brokers that specialize in matching owners and buyer. Talk or meet with a few business brokers. There is limited information available until you sign a Non-disclosure Agreement and a Non-Circumvent Agreement before they disclose the details about the company. This obligates you to keep what you learn confidential and not discuss with employees or other people outside your due diligence group.

The Non-circumvent Agreement protects the broker. You do not go around them and make a deal that cuts them out of the transaction.

These operating businesses may or may not be profitable. The amount of profit, the potential market, negotiation skills, and other factors will determine the sales price. You need to investigate what could be done to improve the business and make it more successful. Consider hiring a couple experts to identify opportunities for a net improvement – extra revenue minus extra costs to get it done. You do not want to buy a mediocre or declining business without having a solid plan to improve the business.

As mentioned earlier, is very normal to not know exactly what you want to do. One thing to do if you are stuck is to read through lists of business types or of jobs that could be a potential business for you. If you are still struggling to find what you want to do, then take a different approach. Go through the list and cross out everything you do not want to do. Going through a process of elimination may help find what you do. There is an 8 page list of businesses on our website to give you ideas.

Something to consider in deciding to start a new business is, have you ever owned a business before and do you know people who will truly support and help you. If you have owned a business before and if it did not work out, did you honestly investigate why it failed? Not use excuses. Can you learn from what did not work? Also know what you did properly and can it apply to this business?

Do you know people who already own a business who are willing to share their experiences and information? If their business succeeded or failed, they may be willing to provide a true insight as to why. This is a tremendous benefit. Be aware their views may be tainted by ego and excuses.

Once you have an idea for a new business, you need to do research to understand if people are willing to pay for what you want to do. It is good if your business idea has lots of competitors. You may love to play tic-tac-toe, but you may have a challenge making money doing it.

DO NOT wait until every product and service is created, until you can afford to buy a building and all the equipment, until you have all the staff, until you have all information, and all the other aspects of your business. You MUST have one or two high quality products and/or services, all the core business aspects done and ready to meet or exceed your customers' requirements.

There are other aspects that you will continue to work on, and become aware of after you start the business. Your current guide will include these as part of a future action plan with an estimated date to implement. You need to always be learning and applying.

As you operate the business you will get ideas and feedback from employees, customers and may be from suppliers. Review them and decide what you will do during startup and what to include in the expansion plan.

Every business is different, even in the same industry. It is like two couples living in the same area taking a trip to the same location during the same time, but unaware of each other's plans. There may be a common method of taking an airplane and staying in a hotel.

The couples will probably fly on a different airline and schedule. There is a very small chance they are on the same flight. One may be going first class and the other economy, or they are near each other. They will probably use a different way to get to a different hotel. Maybe they are staying in the same hotel. During the trip they will do different activities. They may run into each other at some time.

With all the differences, both couples have the same objective (have fun), do some of the same activities (fly, stay in a hotel, sightseeing), and complete the journey (return home). Your business will have common and unique objectives and activities, and maybe you see a competitor at a networking meeting.

It is perfectly normal not to know what type of business to start when you begin thinking of starting a business. There are ways to help you find the type. Maybe you know what type to start, which could change after you do some investigating. You may start the business or buy an existing business or franchise. The business can stay part time or intend to be full time.

Story:

Through my life I had a variety of jobs – or attempts at some. In my first round of going to university, I got involved with selling pots and pans door-to-door. I learned some sales information and techniques, but it lasted a couple months.

I got my insurance license and started with a company. I was assigned to a group that provided health and business insurance to ranchers and farmers. Half of my aunts, uncles, and cousins were involved in ranching and farming, so it sounded okay. I learned about the policies and was uncomfortable with parts of the coverage and the cost.

Then I was assigned a territory to cover during the week. It was a 8 to 10 hour drive leaving mid-day Monday after the sales meetings. There were hundreds of possible miles and the hours of driving time during the week, and back early Friday to complete paper work. At this time in my life, this did not fit and I was not motivated to continue.

I have mentioned how I got into real estate. One reason why I enjoy doing real estate is because it is a high dollar business. One of my worst businesses would be a $1.00 store. I'm a bit A.D.D. and spending my time and effort trying to save 2 cents on a 50 cent purchased item does not motivate me. Some stores have a 4% to 8% profit so saving 4% is a BIG deal. If properly managed, these stores can provide the income and other rewards the owner wants.

These "dollar" stores need to sell thousands of items every day, manage their inventory very closely, and confined to a fairly small space. Obviously this does not bother some people. For real estate you could work on a few deals at a time, that takes a few months, and get out of the office.

There are other reasons why I enjoy real estate. I like the diversity of real estate business types for multiple streams of income, solving seller's or buyer's problems with typical or creative transactions (all are legal), leverage funding, and a big one for me as a "rehabber" is turn a piece of junk into a gem to rejuvenate neighborhoods and provide work for lots of people.

Tip:
Find an accountability person to work with you. Doing the research, creating plans, doing the activities, keeping up the time schedule will be a challenge.

You need someone who understands what you are doing and why, who understands what it takes to accomplish what you are working on, who can see things you do not, and objectively support you.

They are your cheerleader and confidant to share your struggles, but they need to be honest with you and call you out when you are off course or doing something that you should not be doing. It can be difficult for family or close friend to do this.

They may or may not be your mentor or coach. The primary role of mentors and coaches is to help with what needs to be done. The primary role of the accountability person is to make sure you are doing what you are supposed to be doing. These roles can be done by one person, but they need to help with what needs to be done and are you doing them properly.

Look for someone you trust to help you.

Bonus:

If you are stuck send an email to stuck@ lylbusinessdevelopment.com for some free assistance.

Vision, Mission, and other Statements:

"In order to carry a positive action we must develop here a positive vision." Dalai Lama *(Religious leader)*

Once you have a good idea or know what you are going to do, you need to define the business so people understand the direction and intentions of the business. This is one way to differentiate businesses in the same industry.

Vision and Mission Statements are typical ways to clearly and concisely communicate the intentions of the business.

A Vision is a short statement that informs and clarifies why the company exists and what the company will become in the future when it follows the Mission. It inspires and challenges.

For example Walt Disney's Vision is - "To make people happy."

The Mission is a high level of what, who, and how the company will provide the Vision.

For example Walt Disney's Mission is "The mission of The Walt Disney Company is to be one of the world's leading producers and providers of entertainment and information. Using our portfolio of brands to differentiate our content, services and consumer products, we seek to develop the most creative, innovative and profitable entertainment experiences and related products in the world."

Some companies will combine these into one statement like Amazon "Our vision is to be earth's most customer centric company; to build a place where people can come to find and discover anything they might want to buy online."

Some companies have a separate Value Statement which states the corporate philosophy and leadership principles for employees to work by.

For great examples read the Ritz Carlton Hotel and Zappos shoes and clothing for their great core values. Consider what fits your business.

Some companies state some of their core Goals and Objectives. I'll define a Goal as a general guide for making business decisions. Objectives are specific and measurable activities to meet the Goals.

As a guide to create goals, there is an acronym called S.M.A.R.T. These represent Specific, Measurable, Attainable, Relevant, and Time Table. When you expand on each word, this will bring clarity to what needs to be done and when.

For example a simple Goal is to become a Realtor. The Objectives are to study the material, pass the exam, and join the Realtor association. The activities are which classes to take, do the studying, take the exam, and others.

Everyone needs an "Elevator Introduction (pitch)". The "elevator" refers to it being very short because of the amount of time it takes to arrive. I do not like "pitch" because you are not trying to pitch (sell) them. I use "elevator introduction". You are informing them about who you are and what you do to see if it generates any interest. For a small business, this or a version can be written and used in place of the Vision and Mission Statements.

The elevator introduction has a structure that includes who you are, why they should they listen to you, what you do and what is one core problem you can solve, and ask them an open ended question like "How does this apply to what you do?" or some variation of "Do you know anyone that (repeat problem)?".

You need a short 30 second and a 2 minute version depending on how much time you have, where you are, and do they seem genuinely interested in what you are saying. The short one will have one problem and its solution so you "Keep It Simple". The longer one will go into a little more detail and/or maybe includes a second problem and solution. Always open a conversation and ask them what they do. You could find a common interest to start building a working relationship and maybe create a friend.

You need a clear vision and mission to keep you on the right path. The vision is why the company exists and the mission is a high level what, who and how will the Vision be met. Have an Elevator Introduction to let people who you are and what you can do to help others.

Story:

I'm a big note taker and type lots of information into a document relating to a topic. The document has information, screenshots if appropriate, questions, and actions. I'll scan some hand written notes or type the information into a document to find easier. Creating these types of documents is part of the Discovery element of the Process.

My work and "home study" courses involving real estate several decades ago gave me an idea of what I wanted to do when deciding to leave HP. I had a vision and mission, but did not write them down. I'm good at visualizing and taking action (sometimes a bit slow) so I'm guilty of not writing these down.

When walking through a house as a possible investment, I can imagine the work to do by moving a wall, extending part of the house and moving closets, or just doing cosmetic work. I also estimate the cost and think of the 2 or 3 exit strategies. When it becomes a transaction, then I write all this down so it can be given to others to do.

Over the last ten plus years, there have been some major industry related changes so I had to make a few revisions in my goals and objectives, but not my vision or mission.

As you are starting, I HIGHLY RECOMMEND you write down your vision, mission, and a few other pieces of information on a single piece of paper as a reminder.

Writing a book was a goal. The topic was going to involve real estate investing. However, after attending a seminar, speaking with a few people, and a couple other factors, it became crystal clear to start a business to help people do what I did - Working Yourself Out of a Job. It needed to be a guide so I create a process for people to follow based on my previous and current business ownership and my work as business analyst and project manager. This became my book topic, and here is the result.

You can go through the process to find your destination and create a roadmap to get there.

I have another vision with an ultimate goal of setting up an organization to help teenagers and young adults learn about being a business owner and provide resources to take action. Our school system does not provide this type of information. There are some organizations that provide some information and experiences, but not to the degree I want to do.

Tip:

Create, print, and display your one page Pledge where you can see it. It is more than just having some pictures. It is more than your Vision and Mission. It includes the "whys" you are doing this, your UVP, maybe your biggest concern so you can confront it, and a couple rewards.

At this time you probably do not have all the information for this. Enter as much as you can and add more as you progress.

I hear people say having a vision board is a waste of time and does not work. I agree if the person does not have a strong enough reason to start the business and take the appropriate actions to start the business. If you need a change, the vision board will help you keep focused and motivated.

A Dream is just mental stimulation until you take appropriate actions to accomplish it. If you can only Dream today, you must still take actions to create a Plan to someplace. You never know when Mr. or Mrs. Opportunity will come knocking and your Plan becomes a reality.

Business Entities and Taxing:

The following section is specific to the USA. Your country will have similar or different types of business entities and how an individual can do business without an entity. You need to consult experts for the types and registration process.

There are many types of USA business entities and each entity has certain type(s) of IRS tax classifications, and some have corporate reporting requirements. It is a good idea to keep a written record of key business decisions and actions regardless of the entity. Each state has some variations in the entity, registration process and cost to set up each type. For example, the primary owners in a C Corp are publicly disclosed in California, but owners are not disclosed in Wyoming.

Here are the basic types of entities within the United States. There is more information later in the book.

- Sole Proprietor – the owner is not protected from business lawsuits, are created at the county level (some at a state level), is easy and cheap to form, and is not required to have annual meetings or record minutes.

- Limited Liability Corporation (LLC) – created at the state level, independent legal entity so Members (owners) have large amount of protection from business lawsuits, uses an "Operating Agreement", separate business and personal assets, and is not required to have annual meetings or record minutes.

- Partnership – created at the state level, have at least one "general" partner who has unlimited liability for company liabilities and has complete management authority, the "limited" partners do not have any liability beyond what they invested, and is not required to have annual meetings or record minutes.

- S Corp – created at the state level, independent legal entity so Shareholders (owners) have protection from business lawsuits (if regulations are followed), separate business and personal assets, must have annual meetings and record minutes.

- C Corp - created at state level, independent legal entity so Shareholders (owners) have protection from business lawsuits (if all regulations are followed), separate business and personal assets, must have annual meetings and record minutes.

Some of the entities such as a Sole Proprietorship and S Corp have one IRS classification. The LLC has different IRS classifications depending on the number of Members. The LLC can be taxed as a "disregarded entity" similar to a Sole Proprietorship, or as a Partnership, or as a Corporation.

There are pros and cons to each type of entity and the IRS tax classification. What you select will depend on several factors in your personal life and business objectives so you need to consult business professionals. The major factors include your age, personal and business asset protection, current and future income, current and future tax bracket, need for life and health insurance, how much money you need for personal and business growth, retirement savings, and others.

The business professionals include CPA, entity structure, estate planning, retirement savings, and various insurance and other benefits. Some people are an expert in one area and has some knowledge of another area(s).

The reason you need to talk with a few business professionals is to understand the conflicts between them and decide which entity and tax method fits you best. For example a tax professional may focus on short term profits which can conflict with long term estate planning. The retaining of profits for growth and company paid benefits is good in a C Corp; however, there is double taxation of income – business and personal.

You could have different businesses and they could be the same or different types of entities and tax classification. Actually, you could have one entity as an owner or member of another entity. Consider an entity as the general partner in a partnership to reduce personal liability.

The type of entity and how it is taxed is important. There are pros and cons to each so consult various professionals to find what fits your situation the best.

Tip:

Celebrate small wins and completing milestones on your journey to start a business. We are rewarded for good behavior throughout our life. Sometimes we do something well or meet a business objective and it is ignored or belittled. Now you have control.

With the activities involved it will be easy to get consumed. Take a little time to reward yourself. These can be simple and inexpensive. Take the family to a nicer restaurant than normal and let them know it is because of the progress. This outing makes it a reward for you and for the others making some sacrifices. Completing milestones also gives them more confidence you are on the right path.

If you do not have a family, buy (inexpensive) or do something special as a reward and reinforcement. Maybe do the same thing each time so you have an anticipation of doing it again soon. We thrive on positive stimulation.

Chapter 1 Notes

Ideas:

Questions:

ACTIONS:

The DPIE Model

The DPIE Model ™ is a comprehensive and structured process to starting a business. It does not matter if you want a hundred thousand or a million dollar business.

The process is not what gets the activities completed. It is the framework that includes supporting documents to organize all the information and activities to start your business. It is the guide to your destination.

You may have noticed I have used the words "discover" and "plan" in prior sections of this book. This section is about the processes and less about why you want to start a business and what the business is.

The process involves 4 elements that create a circle. Each of the elements has specific and overlapping purposes, information, documents, and activities.

The 4 elements of the DPIE Model:
- Discovery
- Planning
- Implementation
- Expansion

The concept of the process is straight forward – to gather and organize information to identify the activities to perform. **Do NOT** underestimate the importance of the process because of the simplicity. McDonalds is known for its process as a guide for 20 – 30 year old people to manage a multi-million dollar business. We also have supporting documents to create your journey, and take action with other people.

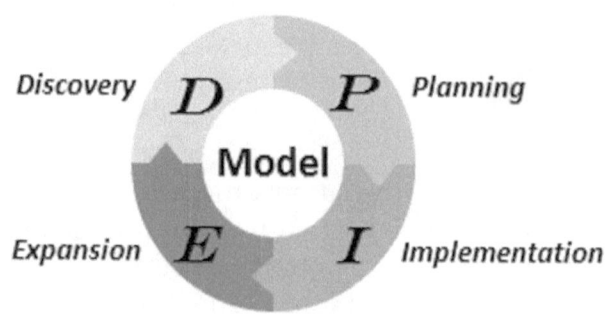

You need to pause or stop the journey occasionally to review the information and ask a few important questions.
- Is this still a viable business?
- Will it provide the rewards I want?
- Is it what I want to do?
- Where do I need help and who can provide?

There is an old saying about not seeing the forest with all the trees. This means you can get so caught up in the activities you sometimes forgot to make sure you are still on the right path. Do not give up when you come to obstacles, but find ways and seek help to get around them. Review your Pledge page with reasons, vision, and more.

Discovery:

"Twenty years from now you will be more disappointed by the things that you didn't do than by the ones you did do. So throw off the bowlines. Sail away from the safe harbor. Catch the trade winds in your sails. Explore. Dream. Discover." Mark Twain (Writer and Lecturer - real name Samuel Langhorne Clemens)

I would like to add: Take action now to pursue your Discovery because time and tide do not wait for you.

A few objectives of Discovery are to understand why you want to take this journey, what do you want to do, and begin to gather and investigate the information you need to start. Another objective is to create documents about the information you gather and prepare for the next steps.

The first part is to understand why you want to start your business. This was discussed in the Your Reasons to be a Business Owner section.

The second part that we also discussed is that you need to understand and realize that having concerns of starting a business are very normal. The concerns can be overcome with knowledge and confidence as you proceed through the process. There will be challenges and distractions so you need to remember your vision, mission, and your "whys" you are doing this.

The third part is either knowing or finding what type of business you want to own. Do you have the knowledge and skills to start and operate a certain type of business? What do you need to learn?

If you have more than one idea, pick the one that you enjoy doing the most, is easier and faster to start, and/or can provide rewards quickly. Trying to operate more than one business at a time will cause distractions and neither of them gets done. You could do a little work on a related business idea that will benefit the primary business work, but still get one business operating before continuing the other.

The fourth is what type of business entity fits your situation. What are the pros and cons to each?

The last is creating various documents with the information, plans, and activities for your business. Also realize you will need help from other people and companies.

The result of Discovery will be a solid idea and several documents of information for your journey. You may know what you want to do, but as you go through Discovery, you might learn it is not want you thought and look for something else.

There are a few documents to create now because you are beginning to gather information and have some activities.

One of the core documents for your journey is a Lesson Plan. This is a combination of general information and outlines what needs to be done with some specific activities. You could enter a summary answer or comment in this document. There is a different document for detail information.

You can create a Lesson Plan as you read this book and do some research. This is one reason each chapter has a Notes page with Ideas, Questions, and **Actions** so you can identify what you need to do. Hopefully you need more space to write these and far more information which leads to the Business Information document.

We have created a Lesson Plan with 12 Modules, over 30 Lessons, and about 100 Activities covering the core aspects of starting a business. It includes some information and questions for you to answer to gather your business information. There will be activities that do not apply to your business and you will add some activities specific to your business.

The majority of the information you gather is entered in a separate Business Information document. This was mentioned earlier in the book when reading the book and you need more space to write Ideas, Questions, and ACTIONS.

The Business Information document can follow the structure of the Lesson Plan, or you organize it in a way that makes sense to you. This is for all the detail information to start your business, and includes lists of ideas, questions and actions related to the information, references to information, and more.

Another document you must create is the Master Plan. This has all of the activities you need to do. The activities in the Master Plan have an estimated due date, actual completion date, status, and comment. A spreadsheet is the best format.

Depending on the complexity of your business, you may need some specialized plans such as Marketing, Operations, and Financial. When you have separate plans, you will have one or few key activities in the Master Plan to represent the separate plans – hence "Master".

We highly recommend you use a Business Journal document to keep track of issues, milestones, and other things you want to remember. It can be daily or weekly or when something happens. It has a summary or a few related details about what you are working on, how much time you spent (overall or on a specific activity), what has been accomplished, what is missed and how do you get back on track, and other comments. It can also include some emotional feelings.

You should continue this or a variation after the startup so you have a record for future reference – great to give to someone if you are having problems with the business.

Here are some benefits of a Lesson Plan, Business Information, Master Plan, and Journal documents:

- Structures the information and activities for awareness and to take manageable steps.
- Allows you and anyone helping you to see what you need to do and when, and track your results.
- Provides a review to make sure you are working on the right activities at the right time.
- Provides discussions for accountability.
- See how much time is being spent on key activities, where are you getting bogged down, and where you can find more time to accelerate your journey.
- Uses information to justify adjustments to your Plan – NOT to the Vision or Mission.

Discovery is just that, find what you want to do, gather and organize information to begin creating the appropriate documents. Some can be very basic with 2 – 3 pages, or more comprehensive depending on the size and complexity of the business, and your knowledge and skills.

Story:

Through much of my life I had the "shiny penny syndrome". I realized numerous years ago it was distracting and is now under control. Jumping around different types of jobs and businesses has led to learning opportunities with some applied in various businesses and jobs. At least trying a few jobs for several months helped decide what I did not want to do and did not waste a lot of my life.

The Discovery section of starting my full time taxi business was an easy evolution. I had been driving part time for over a year while going to university. It worked well because the schedule was very flexible and got paid cash that day. If I had time and needed some money, I'd call the company to get a car for as long as I wanted or occasionally switch car because someone else had it booked.

When I decided to drop out of university, I bought a car and would lease it during the day and the weekends I did not want to drive. I preferred driving at night. I made enough money leasing the car out to pay all my fixed and most of the variable expenses. The majority of money I made was profit.

All industries have niches. Real estate, health, sports, animals, and business are just a few industries. Numerous years later, I did a Discovery while working at HP. This was about what types of real estate to do. Each type has pros, cons, and are suited for certain skill sets.

People may not realize how many different types and niches there are in real estate. Without going into details, I'll categorize real estate businesses into finding, directly involved, passive, representation, and support. There are classifications of properties such as residential, commercial, industrial, and specialize.

Looking at the Residential classification, the niches related to finding is Birddog and Wholesaling. The niches related to directly involved Rehabbing and Landlord. The niches related to representation involve Agents or Brokers. The niche related to passive is Private Lenders. The niches related to support relates to Title Company, Attorney, Inspector, Appraiser, Contractors, and others. Putting these combinations together creates a large number of possibilities.

All of these niches involve knowledge, skills, and experiences to be proficient at doing. Being able to perform a niche is like having another tool in your toolbox. Having various tools is intentional congruency.

As part of my initial real estate Discovery, I spent a lot of time, effort, and expense to build my knowledge and skill set, and talking with lots of people. The result is a large number of tools in my tool box. These were applied to gain experiences. There have been some experiences that none of the people I have talk with have experienced – yes, others have experienced the same or similar, but I have not met them or discussed with people I know.

There are niches I do as my primary business, some I use to resolve a specific situation, some I do when necessary, and some I have no interest in doing.

I have been fixing things since I was old enough to hold a screwdriver, hammer, and other items – before I can remember according to my parents. After graduating university, turning the ability to fix and build things into a part time home maintenance business was an easy decision.

Now I rarely do any of this work. I hire others to do these, but I understand what is involved, speak their language, and have an idea if their pricing is reasonable.

I attend business owner conferences and listen to very successful people talk about what they do and how they can help us. In one of the conferences it became extremely clear I need to use my business owner and corporate knowledge, skills, and experiences to create a new business to help other people start their business.

The timing was perfect because I had freed up a bunch of my time involved in real estate. I have been doing this so long I have many good people performing the majority of the activities. The extra time gave me the opportunity to write this book, create the supporting documents, determine the website functions and a developer finished setting it up, and completing other activities. With these done, the time will be available to work with you and have others to help.

I don't want anyone to have an idea of me starting the business to help other people start their business as a "shiny penny syndrome". I'm not jumping out of real estate. I can do both successfully with the great teams of people.

You need to go through Discovery to identify your industry and niche. REMEMBER, it is normal to not know what you want to do when you decide to start the journey. The Discovery results in certain documents being created and used. Find capable people to assist you.

Tip:

Consider putting the core documents online so you can access it from any computer with Internet access from home, work, or when traveling. For example you can put your Finance Information and Projections documents in a folder and give "edit" access to your CPA. Another person has "read only" access to your Marketing information.

Microsoft OneDrive is good because you can use their online software to edit the Master Plan, Journal, and other documents so it does not matter if you have a PC, Apple, tablet, or smart phone.

You can create different folders to control access to groups of documents. You can also provide "read only" or "edit" access to other people. With OneDrive, the people do not need to "register" or "log-in" to access the folder or files.

Planning:

"Planning is bringing the future into the present so that you can do something about it now." Alan Lakein (Author on Time Management)

I'll use a definition of Plan – the result of a process to identify what needs to be done with a time schedule to accomplish the objective. Let's look at this sentence backwards. You have an objective to start a business. There will be a timeline to start and complete the activities. The activities are determined by going through the process to gather information and decide what business you want to own and what is needed. You create the Master Plan and other appropriate plans.

DO NOT GET OVERWHELMED! A plan may seem complex, but it is just a type of list. I realize coming up with some of the information for the plans can be challenging for more comprehensive businesses or if you lack information. Perseverance is a virtue.

Let's look at a very common type of plan hundreds of millions of people do every week – probably you too!

When you go to the grocery store, you are planning and there is a process to accomplish your objective. The process starts with you deciding what you want to eat. You check what you have and the recipes so you can determine what you need. You get a piece of paper and pen to write down what you need so you do not forget. You may check if you have any coupons. You decide which store(s) you drive to. You may know the store layout so your list groups common items or you meander up and down the aisles looking for items. You will probably change your plan by adding items not on your list. You check out and may drive to another store or go home. You then organize the items as you put them away.

If your planning was done correctly, you met your objective and you have everything you need. Sometimes your plan has a gap and you forget something or you find the item at home has expired and not usable. Then you need to decide if you want to go back immediately, change the recipe or go back to the store later and cook it another day.

You are now ready for the next objective with a process to prepare the meal.

The Planning element is about finishing the creation of plans and your time is spent working on the plans' activities. The trigger to moving into Planning is once you know or have a solid idea to pursue and have gathered the majority of information. During the Planning element, additional plans may be created with specific activities.

I discussed the Lesson and Master Plan in the Discovery section. You create these as soon as you start your journey. The Lesson Plan is a guide for your journey. The Master Plan is the itinerary for your journey.

With more than one plan, each one has a specific purpose. Here are a few other plans to consider. All of these other plans have more details in other chapters of this book.

There is a Marketing Plan to know how to get your messages out effectively. I use "marketing" as a general term in the book, but it involves more. There is a separate section later in the book about Branding, Marketing, and Advertising.

There is a Finance plan with other types of documents. This is an estimate of how much money is needed and when, from whom, how are you going to make the money, how and when are you going to pay back the loans, and other information.

There could be a Staffing Plan which relates to who performs what business tasks, what is the classification (employee or contractor, part or full time), benefits, and other aspects. There are 3 basic business organization levels – Owner, Manager, and Staff. Even a one person business needs to think and act according to each of the level's roles and responsibilities.

A Location Plan involves where you operate and the type of structure. This is not needed if you work from home or if you are renting space and just need to add some furniture and office equipment. The activities can be in the Master Plan. If you are renting space or buying a building and there are a bunch of renovations (build out), then you should use a Location Plan.

An Operation Plan is needed if you have complex processes. The machine shop uses the Location Plan for the location and structure. The Operation Plan is needed to document the equipment requirements, layout, and connections to the structure. This plan will include an activity to create the procedures such as operations, safety, emergency, and regulations. This is very specific work so it belongs in a separate plan.

Your business may be a bit smaller in scope so you could combine the location and operation activities into a plan. For a basic business, the activities are in the Master Plan.

An Expansion Plan is needed if you are intentionally starting the business with a few products and already know there will be activities later. If there are some basic activities over a fairly short time period, then add these to the bottom of the Master Plan.

If you are planning a large expansion such as moving from a small rented building to a large building you own, then create an Expansion Plan with all the activities. If it is a significant change, there could be additional core plans such as Finance, Staff, and Operations. These will have the appropriate activities.

The Business Plan is the last key plan and most people have heard of. It is needed for just about every business. A few people claim you do not need one and in very rare situations I agree. For example, if you are an experienced Realtor and want to create a "team" with a couple other Realtors working from home, then you may not need a Business Plan. If your team is going to have a dozen Realtors, open an office, and need money for startup, then you will need one – even if it is several pages. You will also need a basic Master Plan for all the activities to start it.

The Business Plan takes key information from everything you have done to this point. You organize the information in a different way, but I HIGHLY recommend that you follow the US Small Business Administration's (SBA) organization guideline. If you intend on getting a SBA loan, you must follow the guideline. It makes it easier for the bank and the

SBA to read and understand your information. Even if you use other sources of money, the SBA guideline is a good one to follow. FYI - a SBA approved bank issues the loan, not the SBA. The SBA guarantees the loan meeting certain criteria.

You may be able to create your own Business Plan following the SBA guideline. We can help you create a basic Business Plan. Giving all your information to a reputable company can create a great Business Plan.

There are thousand companies that claim they can write your Business Plan. This is a huge industry because most people do not understand how to write a plan.

Many of these companies can do a great job when they have all your business information, and they have access to related industry information, and market and economic information. Be very cautious if the company just sends you 20 questions to answer. Ask where they get their industry related information. Get examples of other plans they have done and hopefully in your industry. Ask if they guarantee their plan to be SBA compliant and will they do revisions to meet SBA compliance for no additional cost. Do a review search online to check them.

The Lesson, Master, Business, and the other plans with all their activities, time schedule and tracking are the roadmap to your success.

You may need to give other people your plan(s) to perform some activities. You need to omit information about your business they do not need to know about. When someone is working on your Marketing Plan, they do not need to know your Master or Financial Plan. If you have all the marketing and financial activities in the Master Plan, then create a copy and remove all the irrelevant activities.

Before you buy or start a business, have some strategies and triggers to take certain business actions. The strategies involve exit, expanding, reduction, or maybe reach a point to proactively shut down.

Create some triggers that get you to take an action – cautiously if possible or fast if needed. The trigger is based on something reaching a level, or something happening or not happening. You will need to determine what the triggers are and what action(s) to take.

Depending on your situation, you could have an idea of when you want to exit the business and what is the trigger. This could a certain amount of time such as 5 years, reaching a certain age, or the business dropping in value to a certain level.

The expanding would be part of an expansion plan you should create as you begin and operate your business. Expansion needs to be managed so it does not overleverage the business, the proper plans are created and followed, and employees can adjust.

The reduction is part of a contingency plan when the business is not performing due to internal and/or external factors. If you fail in financial performance tracking, you probably will not know what the true problem is and what to fix. You would start cutting expenses, but could be in the wrong areas which can cause bigger problems. Do not automatically cut marketing because it is easier to do.

You might reach a point to proactively shut down the business. When certain triggers are met, the best long term solution is to close. It is better to maintain some resources to start again or move to a better location. It can be very difficult for you and the customers to close, but riding it all the way to zero will never help anyone.

For my rental properties my trigger was its market value dropping 10% and a few economic trend values changing, and/or reaching a certain market value. The triggers were met mid 2000 and I sold my few rental properties to keep a profit. In hindsight and considering the current rise in our real estate market, this was still a good move.

You need to understand your amount of risk, perseverance, commitment, and other factors to decide what strategies to follow and when to make changes.

You have a huge advantage considering you are applying information from this book, and you follow the DPIE Model ™ to create and use the plans and other supporting documents. By gathering all the associated information, you will have the necessary information to implement the start up.

Planning is extremely important. It takes information to create plans with activities to be performed. Some core plans are begun in Discovery because you have activities to perform. Other plans will depend on the type and size of your business. Again, some can be a couple pages and others have many more.

Story:

When I decided to create a Plan B in real estate, I had a 5 year plan to leave my job. I liked my job and made a good salary, and knew it was going to take time to learn a few types of real estate businesses and to find and close on some investments.

When I started the overall US real estate market was skyrocketing across the majority of the country, but only going up a little in our area. The macro and micro markets are different and sometimes they move together and sometimes the opposite. I knew people in the hot markets who would buy a house and in one to three months sell it for 6 figure profits. There were so many opportunities they could do this several times a month if they had the funding.

Our market area did not have anywhere near this number of opportunities with these amounts profits. The first few houses that I bought were rentals in an average price range. During this time it was very easy to get a loan. There were a couple sayings that "if you had a pulse" or "could fog a mirror" you could get a loan. This was true for retail buyers and investors.

You may remember what happened to the real estate market in the mid-late 2000s with the unprecedented number of foreclosures which lead to new laws and regulations. It is now very difficult for a self-employed real estate investor to get a loan, even with a large down payment. About ten years later several banks were fined billions of dollars because of their actions.

I foresaw the Houston area declining so I sold my rental properties to maintain a profit. While the market was in turmoil I continued to learn about other types of real estate niches. I revised what I was going to do and where. This also extended my 5 year time plan to leave my job.

A couple years later I realized the market had stabilized so I began to buy properties again.

It does not take an economic genius to realize the market is going to change again – as it always cycles up and down with flat periods at the top and bottom. However, there are only guesses as to when the next shift will happen and the severity. Some people will forecast the next major shift. A hand full will be right and thousands of others are just guessing or repeating what they "hear".

Create contingency plans and follow the idea of intentional congruency (mentioned in the Introduction – go back if you skipped reading this). Again, these do not need to be complex.

You will probably need to revise parts of your plans at some time. However, do not change your Vision and Mission without investigating what is truly happening and exhausting all methods to get back on track. Guys, learn to stop and ask for directions along your journey.

Tip:

Watch your health. Your health is critical to your holistic life. Be aware of your rest, food, and exercise. If you lose your health it will lead to all kinds of problems in your personal and business lives.

Getting a decent amount of sleep on a somewhat routine basis is very important. Our bodies and mind require this. Some people say you can never catch-up on missed sleep. If you take this literally, then true because you cannot change the past. I have occasionally stayed up all night to study or get work done and may or may not had any slept during the next day. After getting a decent amount of sleep I seem to get back to a normal state.

What and how much you eat affect your body and can affect your mental state. I'm not a nutritionist or a very good example to follow. I eat some good and poor things, and eat less than I did in the past.

Exercise increases your physical and mental state and keeps the blood flowing for energy and proper circulation. If you are dragging at some point during the day, get up and do something active to get the blood flowing to rejuvenate the body and mind for a while.

Implementation:

"Go confidently in the direction of your dreams; live the life you imagined." Henry David Thoreau (Author and Philosopher)

Implementation is when you complete the remaining activities from all the plans and begin operating your business. You may not realize it, but you have already taken the majority of steps on your journey. Look back to see what you have accomplished.

Realize there will be changes to the plans as you begin implementing activities. The less effort you spent in Planning and/or the more complex your business, the more chances you missed something, a key activity needs to be changed, and some estimates are significantly different than actual.

Some of the changes will need to be done during implementation and some can wait until later. If the changes need to be done now, then add them to the Master Plan. Remember to keep focused on just the activities required to start your business and add the future activities to the Expansion Plan.

Don't fall for the "shiny penny syndrome" which can derail your journey at this point.

As you go through the process there is a small chance another opportunity is presented, or you might have an inspiration for a more appealing destination, or maybe a totally different business idea. With the time, effort and resources spent on the current business, do not make a hasty decision. Think very carefully "why" these seem better, is it based on your research and findings or from someone else who benefits from it.

You need to answer some questions very honestly. Does it fit your vision and mission? Is it your passion? Will it provide you better rewards? How will it affect your start date? Will it take more resources and do you have them? Think of other probing questions.

Stop working on everything for a week so you can clear your thoughts. Do some investigating to confirm the other idea fits your vision and mission, and provides better rewards. You will need to make a decision on what to do and move forward. As mentioned earlier, do not work on two businesses at one time.

Implementing is finishing the activities, opening the door, and operating the business.

Story:

I was at a university leadership conference and we did a timed competitive exercise. The objective was to build an unknown Lego object. The students were divided into groups of 5 with two people able to view a finished object for 15 seconds and then go back to our table. Then another two people could go and look at the finished object for 15 seconds. This would continue as long as the team wanted and each trip was counted. This represents the planning to understand what needed to be done.

Once the group believed they knew how to build the object, they would be timed to see how long it would take to build it correctly. If they were stuck, everyone would stop working on it and two people could go back and take a look for 15 seconds and count the trip, return to the table and everyone continue building it. This represents the time and effort to implement.

There was a big twist to this exercise. A couple pieces on the table were not visible when they looked at the finished object so no one knew exactly where they belonged. If they were not visible, then they probably belonged on the bottom. Once you turned over the object they could figure where they belonged due to the shape and size. This represents you do not always know everything when looking and working on something.

Each group's time was recorded when they finished building it. The exercise facilitators would use the number of times your group viewed the finished object and the amount of time it took to build it. This was put onto a chart for them to see the correlation of planning time (number of trips x 15 seconds) and the build time (implementation). It was a great exercise of communication skills and team interaction.

I do not remember all the details, but I do remember that the groups that spent more time planning spent a considerably less amount of time building it, and the total amount of time was less. The fastest team was one of the last teams to start building it. There was about 15 minutes between the fastest and slowest teams.

Tip:

Handle paperwork minimally. Every time you pick up a piece of paper, it takes time to recognize what it is, to read and understand what it is about, decide if or what the actions are, do the action(s) or put it down again, and decide what to do with the paper.

The time could be a few seconds or minutes which is a small amount of time. The issue arises when you have a hundred of pieces of paper lying around and there is no organization. Now you have a mess.

Schedule a specific time once or twice a week to organize the paperwork – even 20 minutes. After this time, schedule another 30 to 60 minutes to take action relating to the paper work. These are different activities so different schedules to prevent getting side tracked going through the paperwork stack. The only action to take during the organization is to discard what is not needed.

Do the organizing more frequently and/or for 30 minutes until the paperwork mess is under control and go back to once or twice a week.

There are different ideas on how to manage paperwork. Here is an idea.

Have different stacked file trays or an accordion type folder to group types of paper work. When the paper is first received, do an initial "Do I need this?" and discard it or put it into a specific tray. During the paperwork review schedule, take the stack from the tray and do a quick prioritize. Some need to be done during the paperwork action time, or put into another tray (still waiting for something to happen before you can take action). File or discard when done.

Go through your files a couple times a year to find paperwork that is no longer needed. Discard the paper or archive it in a box and store out of the work area. Once a year go through the archive boxes to discard paperwork.

Expansion:

"Without continual growth and progress, such words as improvement, achievement, and success have no meaning." Benjamin Franklin (Founding father of USA and Inventor)

This is the growth of your business which actually begins in the Discovery element and continues in the Planning and Implementation elements. This includes both expansion and changes as you grow the business. This creates a full circle to keep you and the business fresh, relevant to your customers, and provides additional rewards.

You set a path for your journey in the Discovery and into the Planning elements. Keep track of new ideas to improve your business and add to the Master Plan for the startup or to the Expansion Plan to incorporate later. You will also learn more about what you can provide and what your customers want as you operate the business.

Expansion includes requested or proactive ideas for new or improvements to the products and services, and how you operate the business. These will probably involve the systems, processes, training, revenue diversification, and others. Be responsive to your customers because you are serving them, to suppliers because they have resources to help you and they want to keep you as a customer, and to the employees who perform the work and have suggestions.

If you are a larger business, consider having a small team with representation from different business functions. They can meet once a month to review all the suggestions to identify ones to investigate further. Maybe there are congruent suggests to leverage for better improvements. If the business is just you or a few people, you still need to allocate time to work on improvements.

Be aware of the possibility and reality of changes to the industry, regulations, economy and others. This goes back to having contingency plans. There could be an opportunity to expand the business or to avoid a negative impact. Hopefully your contingency plans or your reaction can respond faster than your competitors to give you an advantage.

The improvements and expansions will probably require new activities which need to be incorporated in appropriate plans. Try to have all the activities in an Expansion and/or Master Plan. If it is a bigger objective, you need some separate plans such as a Finance or a Staff Plan.

As part of some improvements and expansion, people will need to understand the changes and be trained. There is an established process with systems and tools to help people make changes to their work and adopt the changes. It is called Management of Change (MOC). Most people do some form of MOC and do not realize it. I use parts of the process when I managed projects.

A formal process is intended for major objectives, but pieces of it can be used for a small business. It could be as basic as letting the affected people understand what is changing and why, if or how their work will change, and they buy-in (agree) to the changes. The activities could be in a Master Plan.

It could be more comprehensive with a formal process. Just understanding the purpose of managing changes and having a plan including the people making and affected by the changes is a great part of the success.

When you become complacent, you stop growing. The business can slowly sink and struggle or may not recover. Work on improvements and expansions that are intentionally congruent, and not another "shiny penny".

Story:
I was a part owner in an executive suite and secretarial service for 13 years. We bought a business that leased

6,000 sq ft in a C- class building with 25 individual offices. We would sub-lease an office to a business person so they had an office outside their house and one they could afford. They could use the conference room when they had several people to meet with or did not want them in their office. We had a multi-function copy machine, binding equipment, and did almost all of their secretarial work because it was before personal computers existed. We had and occasionally used a Telex.

There were issues with this location and we wanted to expand. The building thought they could operate the business and the current tenants would stay. Wrong, they all moved with us.

We moved to a 12,000 sqft space in a B+ class building with 44 offices. It was a far nicer building with a parking garage – great to have in during the summer (not 150 degrees inside the car when we left).

Businesses need to adapt to changes in technology, economy, and the industry. Part of our expansion over the years was in office technology.

My wife was overjoyed going from an IBM Selectric typewriter to a Lexitron computerized machine with a keyboard, monitor and a "near letter" quality dot matrix printer. She did not need to use correction fluid to correct mistakes, and she could create, edit, and save letters on this machine. Wow looking back on the technology changes.

When we moved, personal computers had come out (remember the 286 MHz processor with a floppy disk). Several of the businesses had a PC with word processing, a dot matrix printer, and a fax machine. The result was a drop in our secretarial business. We saw a different opportunity with the PC needing dial up Internet and fax machine phone line. We bought a block of phone numbers and PBX so the tenant had to pay us.

The executive suite industry grows the fastest when there is a large increase or decrease in the economy. During economy growth, people moved from their house to our type of office. When they continued to grow, they moved into bigger office space. When the economy drops, they moved out of their bigger space and back to our type of office. If they continue to decline, they move back to their house.

The net result of all the expansion increased our profits. The business still exists today. A person I work with is at one of the locations. Occasionally I meet someone at either of the locations and it brings back memories.

Plan for the expansion and/or improvements in your products, services, location, and other aspects of your business. Some are proactive and some are reactive, think like a Boy Scout – Be Prepared!

Tip:

The routine expenses stay in the primary bank checking account because they are paid during the month. However, set up a few saving accounts. You will be less caught off guard when periodic expenses are due. You do not want to be surprised when these are due and you are low on cash. It may also help reduce your temptation to splurge on things. Use the saving accounts for non-monthly expenses, business improvements, market shifts, and business cycles.

Set up the saving accounts at a different bank so it is less tempting to transfer and spend until the proper time. The expenses include employment taxes, sales taxes, state and/or federal taxes. You may also have license, regulation, professional memberships, and other periodic expenses.

Do not forget your retirement account – great benefit with certain business entities.

You should always be thinking of ways to make improvements and expansion which can take money. You may have an opportunity to buy a competitor or start a related business. If you have a solid business you should be able to get a loan, but rely more on using cash to minimize debt.

Make automatic monthly deposits into the savings account and from the tax refund. Determine the monthly amount for these expenses and retirement. The habit of saving something each month is more important than the amount. Increase the amount as the business prospers.

The economy and markets are constantly shifting so keep about 4 to 8 months of "rainy day" money. Also learn and practice how to live on less money. When you have more money, still be frugal. Don't be like the vast majority of lottery winners with lots of money and end up broke after a few years.

Chapter 2 Notes

Ideas:

Questions:

ACTIONS:

Your Products, Services, and Information

"However, don't let perfectionism become an excuse for never getting started." Marilu Henner (Actress and Author)

There may be a tremendous amount of product commonality within your industry, but there will be differences. All gas stations sell gas, but some also have a store and some do auto repairs. Some have a larger property and lease adjacent space to a fast food business, or another type of business.

All the possible business scenarios in this section are far beyond the scope of this book. The purpose of the book is to help people start a business and it is up to them to decide what they provide to meet their customers' wants and needs.

I'll define what you sell or give away to people into three categories and they can relate to each other – true products, services, and information. For simplicity this book will refer to all three as a "product" unless there is something special to mention about a specific one. There is additional information in the Operations, Process, and Technology chapter.

A true product is a tangible item – something you can see and/or touch. It can be the final product, or used as a component in another product, or integrated with other products. These can range from a pet rock (those who remember this and the great marketing) to a nuclear power plant. There are billions of products.

A service is knowledge or a benefit to someone or something. This usually involves a task that is performed. This includes a trade like a plumber, product delivery, hotel activity, event planner, and a million others.

Information is the imparting of knowledge to others. This grows exponentially and is virtually unlimited. Raw data can be processed to create meaningful information. It can be provided through verbal, written, audio or video content, and with system integration.

We receive information consciously and sub-consciously. It is ignored, or a brief awareness, or acted on now or later. The information can be garbage or lifesaving and everything in between. Information is absolutely critical in the starting and operation of your business.

You could have a business that gathers data, processes it, and is fed into a system for customers to use. The information can overlap as a true product. The information becomes a true product when it becomes tangible and sold or given away.

Each of these is incorporated in your business to some degree. They can overlap when a true product is part of a service with additional information. A CPA has knowledge and software (information) to prepare your income taxes (service), and submits the return (true product).

I've heard several successful people say you do not need to have every piece of information or every product created before you start, and it does not need to be "perfect". What you must have is the primary products, service and/or information. They need to be high quality, and has something better than your competitors so you get recognized.

The sooner you start your business, the sooner you will have revenue to offset expenses, determine if the products are meeting customer expectations, and find and fix any problems quickly. Work on your Expansion Plan to make changes and add new products and services, and to improve systems and processes using technology when appropriate.

The products need to be priced. The price can be based on the competition, your Unique Value Proposition (UVP), service level, your costs and desired profit margin, the economy, and what you might be able to get away with. Some times the price is fairly common such as residential Realtors getting about 2 - 3% for representing a seller or buyer. Some people think that Realtors get all this money, but they are also a business with expenses paid to the State, Realtor boards, broker, advertising, insurance, vehicle, and general business expenses.

Products with the same purpose that many companies provide are called a "commodity". A few examples are hard drive, soda / pop, cell phone service, day care, and the list goes on. These have similar prices. Some commodities can have something very special to sell for a premium price.

Some products are customized and are bid on such as building a new bridge, or negotiated like a consultant managing a project. There is addition information in the book about Pricing.

Changes to your business can include business diversification and leveraging resources into different types of products. If you have a residential construction business that builds a house as a true product and then you refinance and keep as rental so now your service is a landlord. These are congruent businesses. It is not as if you diversify into repairing sailboats.

Your business may be designed to provide different options to some degree so you can serve more customers. Communicate with your customers so you can learn what they want and determine if you can provide it. Your machine shop may have a fair amount of flexibility to build what a customer wants, but you will also have limitations. Try to expand the capabilities to gain more customers.

There is a "chicken or egg first" scenario with the product and the customer. You will have certain knowledge, skills, and capabilities for developing your products. The majority of businesses starts with #1 and hopefully expand into #2.

1. Do you develop the product(s), and then find the customer?
2. Do you take the time and effort to find certain types of customers, and then develop the product?

You must start with one or two high quality product regardless of it being a true product, service, or information. It needs to meet or exceed customers' expectations, but does not need to be perfect (as if anything is). One of the purposes of the Expansion element is to improve and add products.

Story:

WOW your customers with your products and/or services. Most people are accustomed to encountering mediocre or bad service. They appreciate someone going the extra step, a smile, and a kind welcome and goodbye.

Nowadays, it can be difficult or even impossible to find a company's phone number. They want you to send them an email or submit a "ticket" and they may or may not respond when they feel like it. When you talk with someone they could be hard to understand or respond blasé.

At some companies you need to go through 2 minutes on the phone number going through "press 1 for ___", press 2 for ___, ETC, ETC, ETC". Occasionally they have a number for what I want and most of the time you have to wait or figure out how to get to a human because you have a special question. Then the ultimate disrespect for customers is when you get to a point when there are no more options and it says "good bye" and hangs up on you.

A WOW is going WAY above expectations. This is how you build a devote community of customers and advocates or ambassadors for your business. It can be in the form of customer service, a special promotion or event, or an occasional major discount.

You should read about the Ritz Carlton hotel business philosophy, business model, and hiring practice. Every employee is given a $2,000 discretionary budget PER guest to make something right or WOW them. I heard a story about an employee overhearing a guest's wife not being able to get to the beach because she was in a wheel chair. Their employees are TRULY empowerment so the employee worked with others to build a pathway that night so she could go to the beach the next day, and then they arranged a beach-side dinner. The employee did not need "approval" from management to get it done. I'll re-purpose the saying "Putting on the Ritz." to go beyond the getting dressed up to providing service beyond expectations in your business.

Tip:

I want to go back to the topic about ways to improve your products and business. When you hire people with a good mindset and they are trained properly, they are or become experts in their area. Listen to the employees' ideas and reward them. This includes everyone from the line level operator to senior management.

This does not mean that you implement everything they say tomorrow. There needs to be a "process" to review and evaluate the idea according to the mission and goals, factor in existing work, arrange any funding, and create a plan to implement.

Some of the easiest ways to get "constructive" suggestions from employees is to regularly communicate the vision, mission, and what is happening with the business. They need to have a clear idea of what the business is about and working towards. There will be sensitive activities the owner and senior management will not disclose until the appropriate time. With everyone understanding the mission, goals and objectives, this goes a long way to reducing conflicts within and between departments.

At one company I worked for they had suggestion boxes in different areas. I think the HR manager collected them and the management team reviewed them. Our department would make periodic improvements in procedures which may have come through a suggestion.

I heard about people getting paid for submitting suggestions so I assume the process works. I do not know what percentages of suggestions were acted on so not sure how effective it was. Need to give them credit for recognizing the value of employees' ideas.

Another company did not have suggestion boxes, but did listen and act when appropriate. People would be acknowledged and rewarded in quarterly department meetings for achieving key objectives or doing something special.

The managers also had $25. gift certificates that they could give at any time to someone when they did something special. They could give one or more of the certificates at their discretion. The budget for the certificates was an extremely small fraction of the payroll. People really appreciated getting $25 or $50 and a thank-you. Giving someone a $50 raise would insult and make them mad.

Considering most companies want to make improvements to increase revenue and decrease expenses, the cost to reward people to help identify opportunities is insignificant. Some companies will pay tens or hundreds of thousands of dollars on consultants and ignore the people who may have the best ideas. If you are not sure about an idea, then consider hiring a consultant for a second option on employee ideas for a lot less money.

What makes sense to you as the owner?

Chapter 3 Notes

Ideas:

Questions:

ACTIONS:

Competition Analysis

66 "The competitor to be feared is one who never bothers about you at all, but goes on making his own business better all the time." Henry Ford (Ford Motor company founder)

After you know what you want to do or have a really good idea, then learn who is already doing this exact or similar business, and learn from them. Remember the "genius" person.

There is an old saying about "not reinventing the wheel". Spend time researching the other companies and products. Try to understand their marketing message and methods, their target customers, their Unique Value Proposition (UVP), and more about why, what, and how they do things.

By evaluating this you can model what you like and omit what you do not like. You can also find great ideas by being aware of what other companies' do that have nothing to do with your industry. You are not plagiarizing their material, or violating any copyrights and patents, but you can get lots of ideas to incorporate in your business. Ultimately you must have your UVP which is included on your Pledge.

Many people think the competition is the enemy. This does not need to be true. The competition owners and managers can be open, guarded, or closed to sharing information. It depends on how you build a relationship first.

Think how you would react if someone called you and started asking you questions about your business. Would you tell them what your products are, how much you charge, what processes you use, and how you do something? No!

If you come up with a plan to meet these people and build a relationship, then they will probably open up and provide some information.

If you have products or services sold locally, then contact owners in a different city or state. They may feel less threatened if you are not a direct competitor. Do not just call them and start asking a bunch of questions. They may answer some questions but they will stop answering questions and they may not talk to you again.

Before calling competitors, act like a Boy Scout again - "Be Prepared" with a list of questions about general (neutral) and specific (probing) information. Put the questions into a conversation and not like a survey questionnaire.

Do some research to find the owner's or manager's name. Call and ask for the person and introduce yourself. Tell them you are starting a business in (your city) and you are looking for some information. Ask when they have about 45 minutes to talk. Be respectful of their time because they may be busy and they may not want to be rude. They may say they can talk now, or arrange a call within a few days, or whenever they are available.

You should not go beyond the time you set, but continue for a little longer if they are willing. If you run out of time and do not get all the information, ask if you can call them back and maybe set a date and time.

Begin asking general questions about how long they have been in business, why did they get involved, did they buy, start or take over it, and other basic questions. Toss in some generic personal questions like what do you do when you are not working, do you have a hobby, are you originally from (this city) and others.

During the conversation add in occasional specific questions like how many employees do you have, what are a few things going great (people like talking about accomplishments), do you have any challenges (not imply there are any problems), is there anything you would do different, and other probing questions.

Do not ask some questions until you built a strong relationship such as how is the business doing, for basic financial information such as how much do you charge for something, and what processes or procedures are they using.

Never offer your opinion on what they should do, unless they ask and you have some knowledge.

I want to remind you - thank them for their time and sharing with you. If you build a great relationship, they may be willing to mentor you. They could provide information that accelerates your business and you avoid making lots of mistakes.

When I was preparing to start a business, I called a local competitor. I met at her place and we spent 3 hours talking and she showed me around. She answered all my questions, including some I did not think she would answer. I sent her a nice flower arrangement as a token of my appreciation. I called her back with a few more questions.

During Discovery find, join and participate in online forums and blogs. This is a great way to see what people are having issues with and see which competitors are providing solutions.

Some of the forums and blogs are not associated with a specific company so you can become an expert and build a following. Sometimes these sites will let you advertise or promote your business and sometimes there are restrictions so be aware of how you can engage with people on these sites. There is more information in the Branding, Marketing and Advertising section.

Your biggest competitors may not be active and gives you a great opportunity.

Join and participate in local and national organizations directly related to your business and industry or general business.   Build a relationship with people to share information and ideas.

Just about every industry has at least one local and/or national organization. Some of the organizations have a lobbyist looking after the interests of the industry or for the businesses that participate. There will be some differences of opinions on what needs to be done about some topic or issue within the organization. Leave if you do not agree with the overall opinions or do not get any value. Maybe find others who agree with you and start a small group. There are great forums for virtual meetings.

Be engaging and open with others to see if they respond. Maybe it takes a little time to build enough trust for them to open up to you. There can be mutual benefits.

DO NOT GET OVERWHELMED with a couple optional advance methods of comparing competitors or other aspects of your business. These are not complicated to create with some information you have gathered. **The charts below are automatically created after entering some numbers in**

an Excel spreadsheet and picking "Bubble" or "Radar or Spider" chart.

One is a Competitive Analysis chart using "bubbles". Pick two criteria to analyze. Scale each with a relative size circle according to it being bigger or smaller, or better or worse, or other comparisons. The chart has an "x" and "y" axis and if you want to go big, add a 3rd dimension with a "z" axis and a 3D chart. This data is in a spreadsheet and it creates the chart which you can customize a little.

Here is an example of a Bubble Chart with 4 competitors and see how easy it is to visualize some information.

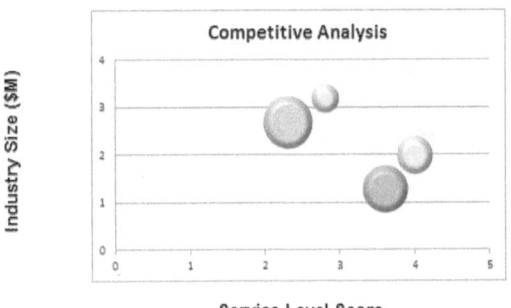

A second type is a Competitive Comparison graph referred to a "radar" or "spider". It has 4 – 12 different factors radiating out like spokes on a wheel. The spokes have a scale. Then identify the value on the scale for each factor for you and each of the competitors. This data is in a spreadsheet and it creates the chart which you can customize a little.

You may want to limit this to 3 or 4 companies, or do more than one chart for groups of companies. Here is an example of a Radar or Spider Chart and see how easy it is to visualize some information.

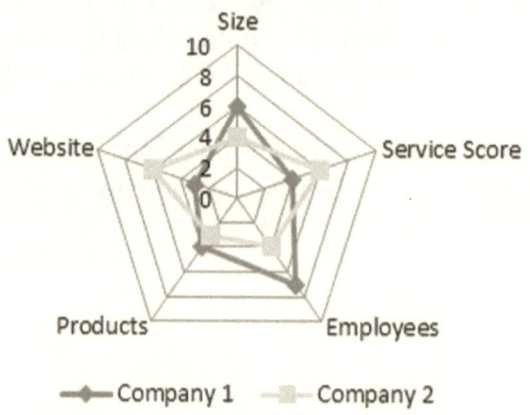

Once you recognize the things you are weak or cannot do, you need to decide which ones you going to learn and provide. Do some research online, ask experts, determine what to add or change and create the plan(s) to implement. Maybe you find a new product or better process to expand your UVP.

Competitors should not be your enemy; they should be a source of information and you build a mutually beneficial relationship. When thinking about starting a business, typically the more competitors means more people buying. You must find your Unique Value Proposition so people buy from you.

Story:

With our executive suites business, we belonged to a national organization with a local chapter of owners and managers. There were monthly meetings that were business and social. Someone would talk about a topic which opened a discussion. We would talk about how things were going with each other and some changes.

We would share information on some topics, but we had to be very careful not to talk about some topics. We did not talk about pricing because we could violate federal anti-trust laws and been fined and go to jail.

Once a year we would get on a large bus, or some people would drive, for a progressive dinner going to someone's office for food, see their place and talk with their employees. The first office had the appetizer, the second had the entrée, and the third had a desert. Every time we did this we went to a different company or location to have fun and learn a little more about our competitors.

There was an annual national convention in different cities. We listened to people talk about industry changes and trends, what some people were doing, exchange ideas, and some fun. At the Washington DC location, we were put on large buses for a scavenger hunt using historical locations and information. Who says you cannot have fun while working, and it met the IRS guideline to be a business trip so a tax write-off.

With us knowing our competitors, we would refer people to them and vice versa. When we were fully leased, we knew who had a similar offices and services that the customer was looking for. Maybe our offices were too expensive, or they needed work we did not have time to do, or it was beyond our capability. Competitors near us would do the same.

We sold the business to a competitor and it still exists today. The original location also exists and the building management leases the individual offices without any services.

Tip:

Take a piece of paper and make three columns and honestly write down as much as you can in each column:

1. What both you and your competitors can do.
2. What they can do and you cannot.
3. What you can do and they cannot.

Look for what your target customer wants or needs that your competitors do not provide or that you can do better. Write these down and make sure you incorporate in your product. Some changes and additions can be done later as part of Expansion. The unique things you can perform that become your UVP which is the core of your Branding, Marketing, and Advertising.

Chapter 4 Notes

Ideas:

Questions:

ACTIONS:

Customer Engagement

" **W**hen you know who your customers are, that can give you an edge on the competition." Alain Bouchard (Billionaire)

You need to determine who your idea customers are. You cannot be everything to everyone. Your product will appeal to certain people or companies. If you repair cars, you are not going to look for people with a tooth problem. Your business has pliers that could remove a tooth, but the pliers have a different purpose, shape and cleanliness.

The people or companies you sell to may be retail consumers, clients, wholesalers, or distributors. I'll refer to all these types as customers. Who you sell to can affect your marketing, pricing, and maybe your warranty. Some of these are mentioned in other sections.

Everyone has a different life experience and situation, but there are some common requirements with different desires. For example many people have a common requirement for a vehicle. Their life experience and situation can guide them to a car, SUV or truck, to a particular manufacturer and maybe a model.

All the vehicles have 4 wheels and get you from point A to point B. Their wants and needs can determine the color, performance, gas mileage, and the all the other possible features. This is why there are so many manufacturers with a large number of models and a massive number of features. Do not think your product will meet everyone's wants and needs.

We are back to the "chicken or egg first" scenario with the customer and product. There was some information in the Product section.

You and/or others have certain knowledge, skills, and capabilities for creating your products. When you are beginning to think about starting a business you probably have not asked or researched your customers' wants and needs.

So how do you know your product will meet their needs so they will buy from you? This is why in Discovery you investigate your product or ideas, you research your competition, you talk with potential customers and ask what they need, and then you incorporate as much as you can to start the business. Add more in Expansion. You will also learn more about your customer needs as you operate the business and these are added in Expansion.

Be very careful not to assume what they want or need.

There are demographics you use to identify the significant and minor attributes of your customers. This can help you focus on the product creation and is used heavily in your marketing. You create a customer profile when you select the attributes and its type.

The attributes and some types for you to consider include the following. You can add others to fit your business. Be very careful not to violate discrimination laws.

- Gender – male, female, or either.
- Age – infant, toddler, young, middle, senior, or a range.

- Physical – body shape (slim, medium, heavy), height, and weight. Some of these are important to a physical fitness related business.
- Appearance – what they wear (shirt, shorts, jeans, casual pants, dress, formal, etc.), jewelry, and others. To a fashion related business some of these are important.
- Ethnic or Religious – whatever their culture or religion accepts. This is not a derogatory attribute because it is based on their beliefs. Many restaurants have fish available on Friday for some Catholics.
- Income – does your price align with your customer, what changes can you do to meet their need or they stretch their financial investment because of the value.
- Education – in grade school, drop out, university degree, professional certifications. Your tutoring relates to one or more of these.
- Housing – own or rent a single family, townhouse, condo, or apartment. Realtors are interested in your current and future changes.
- Location – cosmopolitan, metropolitan, rural, or outdoor. There is an online dating service for farmers and ranchers.

There is a way to visualize your customers or represent your business in a form of logo. Some companies create an Avatar which is a caricature picture. It is a version of "put a face" to your business. When you can look at a picture, it is a powerful way to create a mental relationship.

Avatars are used to represent people on many online websites like Facebook, Twitter, eBay, blogs and forums, so this is not unique.

It can be used as a form of logo like the Michelin Man animation for the tire company or a caricature of Colonel Sanders for Kentucky Fried Chicken.

Take this concept in another direction to create one or two avatars to represent your customers. You may think this is dumb when applying to a customer because you sell to lots of people and they all look different – which is true.

A customer can have some common attributes. There are ranges to the attributes such as age. Your ideal age range might be young adults 20 to 30 years old. Some attributes do not matter, but you still need to pick one for the avatar such as hair style and color, or bald. You want a complete image.

The other attributes to include are gender, facial shape and expression, the color of the skin, physical shape, what they are wearing, if they wear glasses and design, and maybe add a background representing your business or a product.

Having two avatars allows you to use different attributes. One can be male and the other female, light skin and dark skin, skinny and heavier, wear business attire and casual, and other differences.

You can go to a free online Avatar website to either create one or find a picture to upload and transform it. Add this image to your Pledge.

Here is an example.

Sometimes a company will come out with a product that potential customers do not know they want. Apple came out with iTunes so people can download a single song or entire album. Apple did not do market research or customer surveys, Steve Jobs led the company to come up with this and did great marketing to show the features and benefits, and it created a new industry. You cannot expect your business to do the same so learn and understand what your customers need and find ways to provide and exceed it.

There is a movie called Field of Dreams about someone being led to build a baseball field in a corn field for former baseball ghosts to play. There was a line in the movie "build it and they will come". Do not put your business success in the hope customers will find and buy from you. Do some research to determine or have a reasonable idea that people will want it and become a customer. Building a large customer base will probably happen over time and with the proper effort, or it goes viral and builds a base in a very short amount of time.

Customer loyalty is huge. It goes beyond keeping existing customers; it is getting them to be your advocate or ambassador. A great way to build, maintain and expand customer loyalty is to WOW them.

A great example of loyalty is Apple Computer. They have customers standing in line for days before a new product launch. Listen to some of them talk about their device. They stood by the company when Apple's map program had major problems. I know some die-hard Apple users and listen to them talk about the features.

There are numerous other companies or people with loyal customers. Many will also stand outside for long periods of time to get tickets or access. Look at popular entertainment events such as sports, concerts, and plays. You may or may not want to have this level of customer engagement.

When you begin you may need every customer. You will come across customers who are challenging to work with and some will not pay you. Therefore it is okay to breakup with some customers that do not recognize your value or consume so much of your time it affects other customers. Look for ways to do it professionally being tactful, polite, and firm. There is a saying about burning bridges. You may not want to blow up the bridge, but a small burned section of the bridge can be repaired.

The purpose of your business is to provide a product that people or companies want or need. They become a customer when they buy. You need to identify attributes about them so you can determine how to communicate your message to find them easier and they understand your product will help them. You need to continue your support of them or they could go to a competitor. Go beyond expectations so customers become advocates for your business.

Story:

As an investor and Realtor, I work with different types of customers – investors (professional or newbie) and retail (owner occupied). There are conflicting objectives when they are selling or buying. Both types of sellers want to sell for the most amount of money or they are motivated to sell for less. The retail person typically buys a house in good condition and pays a market value. The investor needs to buy it cheaper so they can make a profit.

One big difference between the types of customers is the seasoned professional investor can buy a house that needs major repairs and renovations so they can buy it at a bigger discount. Depending on where the house is located, most have the ability to have work done cheaper than a retail person. A retail person I was representing needed to replace the HVAC system and they got a quote for $7,000. I called a company that I use and they did the work for $3,800 and a better warranty.

A newbie investor who has not built a complete team of people and has less experience will want a house that needs minor repairs and will typically pay more because it is in better condition. They may also pay more because they are not as good at negotiating.

The investor needs a discount to factor in all the costs and make a profit. Investors need to consider what the target customer likes and wants, and what is common or WOW items in that market area. However, many people do not know everything they want until they see something or are aware of something.

When I investigate a property, I decide if it is going to be a rental or immediately resell as a flip. This can determine what repairs or renovations are done and the corresponding cost. Rentals are usually repaired or renovated less than if the property is being sold. I have a couple exit strategies and a customer in mind.

A house I bought was used for crack and prostitution. This area was near a hot market and a couple other houses had been renovated and sold for a relatively high amount. I took a little risk with the strategy to add onto the house for more living space and do a complete renovation. I had a target customer of a small family or young professional. All the objectives were met with turning the junk into a gem, a young couple moved in, and I made some money. The biggest reward was when the neighbors and police officers (who were called in the past because of the crime) came by appreciating what was being done.

Within your business, who are your customers?

Tip:

There is a point worth repeating. Treat your existing customers very well. You spend a tremendous amount of time, effort, and resources to find them and get them to buy from you. It can cost 5 to 10 times more to find them than to keep them.

Yes, there will be customers that are a pain to work with. You may get to the point you tactfully fire them and it can cause some short term grief.

WOW your customers when you can. Go beyond to make them your advocate.

Chapter 5 Notes

Ideas:

Questions:

ACTIONS:

Business Functions

F irst, a reminder I'm not a tax, entity, or financial expert so the following is based on my experience and for general information. Consult various professionals about these aspects of your business.

The remaining chapters are the key business functions every business needs to some degree. Depending on the type, size and complexity of your business, these can be very basic or comprehensive. As you go through Discovery and into Planning, you will understand what is involved.

These functions involve various aspects and are discussed in more detail in the following chapters.

- Branding, Marketing, and Advertising are how you create and communicate your messages about who you are and what you provide.

- Human Resources is the classification of employees, the roles and responsibilities, outsourcing jobs, and following regulations.

- Facility and Location are where you work and do you rent or buy.

- Operations, Purchase, and Logistics are how you create, produce, and deliver your true product, service, or information.

- Processes, Systems, and Technology are the elements of how the business operates and how all the functions are integrated. Some are completely automated, some are done by people, and some are a combination.

- Finance, Accounting, and Measurements are how information is gathered to record, analyze, control, and keep score in the business. The information is used internal by the company and some is provided external.

There are functions with similar business aspects, but different objectives. For example Operations and Finance functions both have aspects that analyze, control, and report performance. Operation's objective is to build the product. They track production tolerances, flow rates, and quality standards. The Finance objective is to make sure the business has the funds it needs, the financial budgets are in line with actual, and is the business profitable. They track information from the financial statements.

The functions can overlap. Operations needs Finance to meet their funding requirements for maintaining or buying equipment, the cost of inventory and supplies, and other expenses. If Operations did not have the funding, it would perform poorly which ultimately negatively affects income and cashflow, which affects Finance's ability to do funding. A vicious circle.

There are ways to have the functions work together more effectively. One is to have a vision and mission that are clearly understood by everyone. Each function needs to have clearly defined and communicated policies and procedures. Hire and train great employees and not just give them a desk and say call me if you have any questions. Together these reduce or eliminate confusion and conflicting business work.

I already mentioned these functions can be very basic or comprehensive. When I was working on my business degrees, there were several text books for 1 function with hundreds of pages – I had 6 text books just on Finance and Accounting. It is impossible for this book to go into the details of each function. Let's look briefly at each of the functions and what are key aspects for you to include.

Branding, Marketing, and Advertising

"G reat companies that build an enduring brand have an emotional relationship with customers that has no barrier. And that emotional relationship is on the most important characteristic, which is trust." Howard Schultz (CEO of Starbucks)

For simplicity throughout this book I use the word "marketing" for a general representation of this business functions and will use this word for its specific purpose when appropriate. These three aspects are discussed later in this chapter.

Marketing is usually the least understood of all the business functions. This is why this is the one of the largest sections of the book, yet it scratches the surface of what you need to do.

Marketing is a challenge because there are so many differences in your customers, unknowns in what to do, creating the messages, what content to use for each communication method, and the cost to create and run. Then hoping you get a 3-4% conversion with some methods.

Many owners and managers underestimate the importance of marketing, so when the business starts dropping they usually reduce these expenses, when they actually should be improving the message and doing more.

In reality you need to know how every aspect of the business is doing so that you know which expenses to reduce, before marketing. We'll cover "knowing your numbers" later. You may want to increase your advertising when business drops so customers remain aware of your business and products. You have an opportunity to increase business because the other companies will follow the path to reduced their marketing and visibility.

Effective branding, marketing, and advertising are an asset and investment in the business. Poor branding, marketing, and advertising are a liability and a waste of money.

There are hundreds of books and thousands of companies involved with all the marketing aspects. For the majority of new owners, you need to complete the business startup process so that you have the proper information to give to marketing experts for them to analyze, provide recommendations, and take actions.

You need to understand the three aspects so you know what they are and can discuss what you want, have an idea if their suggestions fit your objectives, understand the tracking results and testing process, and know there will be adjustments. This is probably why so many owners and managers do not understand how to do these.

Your business will have commonality and differences involving these three aspects with other businesses within and outside your industry. Everyone has the same objective of creating and getting their message out to find and keep their customers. Some of your message and methods are the same or similar; however, you must have and communicate your uniqueness.

With information gathered during the startup process, you must have a Unique Value Proposition (UVP) so people need to buy from you – remember customer loyalty. Your UVP is ingrained in your Branding, Marketing, and Advertising.

Branding:

Branding is strategic about who you and the business are, why you exist, will you love us, inform potential customers you have products and/or services available, will they recommend me to others, and other higher level purposes. It is not about buying a specific product or service. It is to build loyalty to you and to the business and is the umbrella for Marketing.

Branding is about you and the business. In a small business you are representing your business, so you should be branded in conjunction with your businesses. People can become customers because they like you, you can build a relationship and a degree of trust so they will follow and support you, and you need to be true to them. All of this leads to loyalty.

Your staff needs to have a mindset and be trained to building relationships with potential and existing customers so they follow you and the business. Have you ever call a company and ask for a specific person because they were great at helping you, or you wish you could find someone to call?

It uses information from your vision, mission, values, and your elevator introduction.

This includes your business name, logo, a professional looking website, and higher level messages. The brand message relates to information about you personally and the business. It adds a little detailed information to create a clear understanding of who you are and your business purpose. The personal and business versions must be congruent.

Marketing:

Marketing is tactical and has three parts – know your customer, know your product, and the related messages you want to communicate. It is to promote to potential and existing customers so that they understand how you and your product helps them and therefore they will buy from you. It relates to and is consistent with the branding purpose and message.

Marketing is a dialog with both your potential and existing customers. The messages can communicate how your product will fill their needs or solve their problem, the product features and benefits, stories about good things you are doing and how it has impacted people, special offers, and others.

You can have variations in messages. This is to engage certain target customers and involves where and how the message is being communicated. A TV ad being broadcast is going to be different than a letter being mailed. This involves how much time they have. You may have five seconds to capture their attention on a website, or they need several minutes to read an article, or several days to read a book. With the variations, the messages are always congruent.

In the Customer Engagement chapter, I mentioned customer demographic attributes such as gender, age, and others used to create profiles and visualize with avatars. In this chapter you start with one or two ideal customer profiles and look at your avatar to begin conversations to understand their wants and needs. What pleasure can you add or pain can you remove.

Talk with people you know or to people that they know who are interested in what you are doing. Talk with people at network meetings, parties, and other places. You use your elevator introduction to open a conversation and find potential customers. If they are interested, go through some predetermined questions to understand how your product could relate to them, if they are using or doing something similar to yours and by whom, is it meeting their expectation, what is missing, and other questions so you can learn if your product meets some or most of what they need.

The questioning needs to be done in a friendly conversation and not make it sound like you are drilling them. Your questioning should not last more than 10 or 15 minutes to avoid smothering them. They could be being polite and not really care or they lose interest. If they are really interested, you can continue the conversation a little longer or at another time.

There is an art and science to creating messages that attract people to become customers, and for existing customers to buy repeatedly. The art side is the use of creative elements to attract, capture, and engage people appealing to their feelings and intuition.

The science side is the use of technology and research to reach people by understanding their needs and problems. This side is getting stronger and easier to use than in the past because of the very rapid growth of technology that makes information available about people.

There are great debates about which is most important. I believe people respond to both so you need to try different degrees of art and science for your messages and find what works best for you. This gets into "split testing" that is mentioned later.

There will be shifts in what people need and their problems, but basic human nature of having needs and problems will not change. There can also be shifts in your customers. The shifts can occur slowly or quickly so your message needs to change accordingly. The shifts are not announced so you always need to track your results and recognize when something is not working as anticipated.

Some of the shifts are caused by people aging, changes in income, where they live, and others. Some of the shifts are caused by your product changes and/or new ones. You need to understand more about your customers and you find ways to provide what they need. Go back through your contacts to find people you have not spoken with for years, they may now have a need or know someone who does.

For example a year ago someone was not interested in your lawn service because they lived in an apartment. They buy a house and now they want to do some landscaping so they hire you for a one time job. In a couple years they get tired of mowing the grass so they hire you to cut the grass on a regular basis. There is a shift in needs over time.

A local company started as a residential pest control company. Over the years they added other services such as lawn maintenance and landscaping, pool service, HVAC, and security. They expanded these for commercial customers. They expanded into other cities so their market area has changed. Their brand expanded. The marketing and advertising has dramatically changed over time and they may change parts of the message content depending on the city.

Advertising:

Advertising is very tactical about getting your messages out. It is the content and methods to communicate the messages from the marketing. All messages must be clearly written so the people seeing or hearing it feel and respond the way you intended – even if they are not aware of doing so.

For advertising you need to determine the best ways to reach them. An ad must have a purpose so people are impacted and motivated to do what you want them to do such as be aware of your product, buy your product, contact you, go someplace, or other purposes. The ad must have some combinations of information, evoke an emotional response, an offer, and a call to action.

Understand that most advertising effectiveness is difficult to measure. The advertisement can have various ways to help determine how effective it is. Some ways to identify the message involve contact information such as a special phone number or use an extension number, email address, or an online webform going to a specific database.

Some other ways can include specific content such as a header, message, or tracking number. Another easy way is to ask people how they found you or if someone referred you; however they may not remember.

The effectiveness could be measured by sales through a tracking method in the order management or payment processing systems. You know your base inquiry and sales amounts and see an incremental increase.

There are major communication methods such as print, online, broadcast, and social networking which is becoming a prominent method. There is some overlap like social Facebook being online and broadcast radio being online. Each type has pros and cons so you need to determine what works best for you. Then measure and adjust when necessary.

The print types to consider include business cards, letters, postcards, brochures, trade journals, vehicle magnetic signs, and many others. Some ideas for bigger businesses are major magazine, local or national newspaper, vehicle wraps, and billboards.

Online includes website, email, social (some), and some broadcasts like Pandora, podcast, video and/or audio conferences. Websites have various types of information and can include offers, pay-per-click, digital products, blogs – forums. Email one of the most prevalent ways of direct communication; however, there is a problem with all the scams and spam emails.

It is getting to the point that most businesses need a website, even with one page with some business information and contact information. The type of business, products, and how computer savvy your customers are will determine how simple or complex your website is.

The content should touch all three levels – branding, marketing, and advertising. The domain name should include or relate to all or part of your business name, or what your product is. If it is taken, try to shorten it or add something to make it unique such as a location.

Broadcast includes TV and radio by air, cable / internet, and satellite. These are still extremely popular with certain types of businesses. Some of these ads are affordable in smaller markets, off peak time, and run a several times in a blitz. The question to ask – Do my potential customers watch or listen at this time? How long will it take to build awareness or is my offer very compelling to run it a short time?

To do these right is probably too expensive for your business in the beginning. Companies will spend up to

$4,000,000 for a 30 second ad during the Super Bowl. Now if you consider there are 111,500,000 people watching the Super Bowl, then the cost per view is 3 ½ cents – very cheap per viewer but expensive to pay for. Also did it meet your objective?

The social online has becoming more mainstream with companies like FaceBook, Linked-in, and many others. The majority of them started as "personal" and did not allow business use, but this has changed and there are now ways to advertise on FaceBook and Linked-in, and others.

Social is about personal contact. This involves face-to-face conversations, phone calls, personal emails, and others. You are building relationships that involves branding and marketing so people know who you are and what you do, and advertising the product.

Design a logo that is distinct and appealing. It should represent the business name to make it easier for people to relate it to you. To have something that does not relate to your business could cost a massive amount of money and time for people to associate it to you - Nike spent mega millions of dollars when it started using the swoop logo. Do you have this amount of money? Keep it simple and relatable.

Major companies spend multi-millions of dollars researching customers, creating their ads, and running them. They do not spend this amount of money for fun. Pay attention to what they do for ideas you can use. I am a bit weird keeping a folder of various advertisements that catch my attention and use for ideas. I also pay attention to some TV ads to think about why they selected this message, why did they use this form of communication, I wonder how effective it is, and what I would incorporate.

There is a TV ad emulating an interview that I find very interesting. The owner is sitting with someone who appears to be a TV host. The host is asking questions which promote the business. There are some elements I would keep and a few I would change.

There are ways to get free or cheap advertising. Provide exceptional service so customers become advocates like Apple, social media, news stories, contribute to blogs and forums to become recognized as an expert. Maybe you can advertise on free classified websites.

Use your Discovery work to understand your customers. I mentioned the use of customer avatars to visualize your typical customer(s). Learn the advertising methods related to what they use to find information. If they are internet savvy, then find which online methods they use and how you can advertise there. When customers do not use the internet, do they use broadcast or print methods.

If you are not sure which of these methods to use, find out what your competitors and related businesses are doing, and keep your eyes and ears open to get ideas. Some of this can be learned by networking with your competitors in trade organizations, conferences, going through their website, getting on their email list, and other ways. I mentioned earlier in this book about our executive business service and the information that we learned from our competitors and trade organizations, and they learned some things from us.

There is an old marketing adage that your communication needs to touch someone about seven times to become recognized enough for them to potentially take action. Not everyone needs your product, but they recognize it and maybe pass the information on to someone else or they need it later. Depending on your message, the communication method, and customer interest, the number of touches can range from first time to several times to never. Being successful on the first or a few touches can be the result of compelling message, relationships, referrals, and networking.

Think about yourself and how often you see or hear of a new company and you may not pay much attention at first. Then you see or hear it again, and again, and then you start to consciously think about it. Then you see or hear it a few more times and then you realize you want it and take action. There are ads you could see a hundred times and it does not meet a need so you do not take action. Maybe a year or two later it does meet a need and you buy it. This is the power of keeping in touch.

Use your advertising to entice people with offers including your key customers. They are loyal so reward them with something unexpected. It can cost you 5 – 10 times more to get a new customer than keeping one. It bugs me when companies make a special offer to new customers. I guess they take existing customers for granted. NOT a good idea.

You need to test to find what works. Split testing is having two ads and one communication method, or one ad and two communication methods. You send and track the results, then change "one" thing relating to the content or to the method and re-run to see if it gets the same, better, or worst result. Then change "one" more thing and check the results. Keep the tests small to reduce cost, and the speed and complexity of the analysis. There are some marketing systems that allow you do certain types of split testing very easy.

CONTINUE this cycle until you find an effective message going to the right people in the best methods. Yes, this consumes time and money, but when you find it, it can catapult your business. HOWEVER, do not get complacent; continue to track and make adjustments if the results fall below expectations. Occasionally try something very different. Look at the huge companies and how they periodically change the ads so people do not get bored and lose interest.

If the Marketing department did a "perfect job", then you would not need Advertising because the public would demand that every store stock it, restaurant serve it, and referrals pour in. Then if the Branding department did a "perfect job", you do not need Marketing because of the extreme public awareness and advocate demand. This is not real, but an interesting concept to work toward.

All of your work involving the three levels is used to create your Marketing Plan. It is one of the key plans. It could be a fairly basic with 2 or 3 pages done by you or outsourced to someone. If you plan to create a bigger business, the structure is the same but it will be a far more comprehensive and definitely need experts. Beside experts in your industry and business, get ideas from totally different industries and businesses.

A great benefit of going through the startup process is you have a gathered a tremendous amount of information, insight, and expectations about your business. Knowing who you are, what you do, and what you need makes it far easier for the experts to understand so your Branding, Marketing, and Advertising are more effective.

Branding, Marketing, and Advertising are extremely important, but are usually the least understood of all the business functions. There are so many factors to consider and it can be a challenge to measure the effectiveness. You need to understand that these need to be congruent and be the LAST expense to cut (trim is okay) when the economy is falling.

Tip:

Be disruptive in your some of your marketing – being different gets noticed. Some say bad press is still good press, but it really depends on your type of business and what your customers respond to. Some entertainers can to do stupid activities and still get work and have fans. Some radical businesses can also get away with radical activities and messages such as a rowdy bar. Conservative businesses need conservation activities and messages such as a family restaurant.

If you have the same basic message and use the same advertising methods as all your competitors, how will people know who are and why should they use your business. Create your UVP for the messages. Following what your competitors do is okay if it is effective, but do not blindly follow the herd.

This all points to the fact there is no one way to do Branding, Marketing, and Advertising. Pay attention to what others are doing within and outside your industry, test an idea for a little while and tweak it and test again for a little while. Find what works best for your business, make changes periodically to keep it fresh and not fade away, and be disruptive to the degree you can benefit from it. There are people and companies that can help you.

Story:

Apple had a very disruptive (and effective) ad in 1984 that not only marketed a new computer, but also highlighted that Apple is "disruptive" as a company. The TV ad had gray dressed zombie like people marching into an auditorium and sitting in front of a massive screen.

They were watching a propaganda message when a women in red and white comes running down the aisle swinging a chain and ball. She keeps spinning it to gain speed. She throws it into the screen to smash it and stop the propaganda message.

The message was Apple is not the same as all the same as other PCs. (My editorial opinion is Apple was also saying that PC users are like zombies following the typical PC propaganda.) Today, look at the loyal community of Apple customers. How often do people camp out for multiple days to buy a new non-Apple product?

I was told a story of a small drill bit manufacturer going to a large industry show. They talked with various people to strategize what their UVP is and how could they stand out. The result was a new marketing message and advertising. The herd of companies had pictures and information about their bits on their banners and brochures. This company put a slogan on their banner – "Drill deeper for less" with a little information and not a single picture of a drill bit.

The companies send information to the conference coordinators in advance for the conference magazine and supporting information. The coordinators saw this company's slogan and it caught their attention. They contacted this drill bit company and they ended up on the cover of the magazine and they had a feature article inside.

Why, because the drill bit company was disruptive and caught peoples' attention. I do not know if this was effective with the conference attendees and if it led to more business. It provided the best type of marketing – large exposure, credibility, and it was "FREE".

Chapter 6 Notes

Ideas:

Questions:

ACTIONS:

Human Resources

"You get the best effort from others not by lighting a fire beneath them, but by building a fire within."
Dr. Bob Nelson (Author of Employee Motivation)

The overall time to start the business will be less if everyone keeps to the vision, mission, and objectives to avoid conflicts. Everyone has different life experiences, skills, and mindset, so one person may think of something that another person did not or has a better way to do something. Every person needs specific responsibilities that they are capable of doing. There should be some accountability for each other's work to make faster and more effective progress.

Depending on the type of business, the roles and responsibilities, the number and the classification of people working for or with you, the organization structure, and other factors will determine how much Human Resource work is needed.

As owner(s) of certain types of business entities, you have very little HR work. If you own the business as a Sole Proprietorship, a Limited Liability Corporation taxed as a "disregarded entity", a Partnership, or S-Corp, then the profits go on your personal income tax and there is no W-2 required. You may receive or give 1099 statements. Some require a K1 form to go with your tax return.

If you are the owner of a business set up as a Limited Liability Corporation taxed as a "corporation", or a C-Corp then you will have some or a lot of HR work. You must comply with laws, regulations, including filing W-2s with all the associated information. This takes special knowledge and work so it is usually best to find someone to do this work for you.

We'll define a "role" as the work that needs to be done relating to a business aspect or goal. It groups types of work together to operate the business. The amount of work for each role and size of the business will help determine how many people are needed to get all the work done. The information is used to create job descriptions.

The "responsibility" is to hold the person accountable for doing their tasks. It is critical that employees know their job description and what they are responsible for, to avoid confusion about who is doing what, and prevent over lapping and gaps in the work. This is also the foundation for periodic and annual performance reviews and possible adjustments in work habits and training. It can also lead to promotions, demotions, or leaving the company.

A "task" is a piece of work that needs to be done. You need to decide what you do, what is done by people inside the company, and what you contract or outsource. This will change as the business grows. If the business has several people then you need to define the roles and responsibilities to assign the tasks. The more employees you have, it becomes extremely important or critical to define the roles and responsibilities to assign the tasks.

If you are the only person in the business then the roles, responsibilities and tasks are you.

An example of a role is Bookkeeping with the tasks of reconciling bank statements, preparing invoices, entering accounting transactions into the general ledger, paying bills, and others. In a bigger business with several employees, John's tasks are to post the entries into the general ledger and reconcile the bank statements. Susan's tasks are to prepare the invoices and pay the bills. They are responsible for their tasks. Someone is their manager to make sure the tasks are done properly and on time.

For this book I'll use three classifications of people – employees, independent contractors and outsource. Simply stated, employees have a job description, are on an organization chart, and you have full control of their business work.

Independent contractors have a contract to identify what they responsible for, are not part of the organization chart, and you do not have full control of their work, work hours, vacation, and other factors. The US IRS has defined what you cannot control, but you may be able to influence some of this occasionally. If you have a major project deadline and the contractor is working directly with you, then they need to work similar days and time as you. Maybe they are supporting you so they can work different times or days, or at night and not affect your deadline.

Outsourcing has been going on for thousands of years. It can be similar to an independent contractor in that you have a contract, they are not part of your company, and you do not have control of their work hours, vacation, benefits, and other factors. The biggest difference is there is no IRS definition so that you could have more control and influence depending how the contract is written.

In the last decade many people think of outsourcing as moving tasks to people or companies in other countries. In reality it is having a person or another company do tasks for you regardless of where they are located, including suppliers and OEM.

There is an IRS guideline to know when a 1099 is or is not required. There is no 1099 required when contracting with a company, and when the work is done outside the US and by non-US citizens. Consult a professional to know what to do.

Part of Discovery is to create a HR Plan if you plan to have any employees, including yourself in a C-Corp. The plan includes defining the roles and responsibilities, how many people are needed, the organization structure, what types of jobs (roles) are needed, the job descriptions and the classification. Your HR company can work with you to create this.

There is no simple way to find employees who will be a great asset to the business. You and others in the business or recruiters can interview and screen people, but you never know until after they have worked for several weeks or months. One idea is to hire them on a fixed time contract and then you have the option to hire them full time. This is an easy way to let them go if it is not working out, but some employees will not accept this because of the risk they do not get hired and may lose out on another opportunity. Another is to hire them on probation with the ability to let them go later. This can be a little trickier to let them go. With the probation, consider paying some severance to make a clean break.

When you have employees there are a bunch of HR requirements. These requirements are constantly changing and there are severe penalties for not complying. Who is going to manage the HR work?

I HIGHLY recommend that you hire a professional Human Resource service company. You can hire an experienced person to manage the HR work when you get bigger and the cost makes sense. They need to keep up with all the changes in regulations so you could outsource some HR work such as Payroll to a CPA or certain financial companies. These companies do not do the HR tasks of hiring, fire, and work with employee problems.

We'll use three basic job position levels - 1. Owner, 2. Management, and 3. Staff. Each of the three position levels has different roles with responsibilities so the thinking and actions will be different. I'll refer to all of these as employees.

If you are the only person in the beginning, you will do all three. If you have other people in the beginning, then each person must be assigned to a role with certain responsibilities. Many businesses struggle or fail because they get so involved in the Staff work that they ignore the critical work of the Owner and Manager.

As the Owner, you are the visionary, think about the future, define the strategy, work on key relationships, direct the management, approve strategic changes and resources, and understand and monitor what is happening to make sure everything is on track.

The Management takes the vision, mission, strategy, and goals and directs the Staff. They understand what is happening at a higher level of detail so they can direct the Staff and provide summarized information to the owner. A primary role of manager is to remove or find solutions to Staff obstacles.

They should help decide what needs to change if something is off track. Their thinking is about how they can use the resources available to them to get the work done properly and understand what is needed to expand. They may have approval to do changes up to a financial limit.

You may be starting your journey from a Management level in your current job. Managers can also be dissatisfied with working at a company and what to start their own business. They could have an easier time doing the Management work. Depending on the number of employees and the type of work to be done, they may perform some Staff work.

The Staff are the lower hierarchy level employees. They are just as important in the business as the Managers. They perform their responsibilities with direction and performance reviews by management. Management should listen to their ideas for various types of improvements and expansion.

You may be starting your journey coming from a Staff level in another company. You have been trained to do your work and depending on the size of the company, you may not know very much about other business functions. You must realize you will be involved with a few business functions.

Understand the value of your time. Your work may be worth $100 per hour so hire someone to do the $10 to $40 per hour work. Having a true business is leveraging the employees', contractors', and outsource companies' time and effort.

Keep the organization as flat as possible. You do not need managers reporting to other managers until you have numerous employees. A common guide is 8 staff to 1 manager, but the type, complexity of work and the skill of the staff can adjust this down or up.

EVERYONE needs to understand the vision, mission, and strategy of the business so that they make better decisions in performing their work. How many times in your present job do you wonder why one person or department does something that conflict with another person or department? How many departments arguing about what to do and how to do it? A clearly understood vision, mission, and goals will eliminate the vast majority of the disagreements and be a huge advantage to a small, well run business.

You need to read about Sir Richard Branson's business model. He sets up small businesses with a clear vision, mission, goals, and objectives. He empowers the management and staff to make decisions to run the business. He has reporting processes to track the businesses and actions are decided if off course. The companies are not subject to a constraining bureaucracy so they can respond to opportunities and threats quickly and efficiently.

At this time we'll assume your business is just you. It is extremely important you spend time efficiently working in each position level. The percentage of time will change as you go through this process. Below is a guide on how you divide your time through your journey. If you have one or more other people working with you, the percentages are about the same, but the work is split between the people according to the defined roles.

During the Discovery element your time is about 70% as Owner, 10% as Management, and 20% as Staff. The Owner does the strategic parts of the Lesson Plan with what you are going to do and creating the business. The Management is keeping Staff working on the proper activities. The Staff is working on the detailed parts of the Lesson Plan, updating and adding to the Master Plan, Business Information, and Log, and other support documents.

During the Planning element it changes to about 50% as Owner, 10% as Management, and 40% as Staff. The owner is still reviewing and adjusting what needs to be done and when they are due. The Management is still tracking the startup work and reporting to the Owner. The Staff has more activities.

During the Implementation element and after you begin operating the business, it changes to about 15% as Owner, 35% as Management, and 50% as Staff. The Owner will make minor adjustments and make sure the business is following the mission. The Management has more activities to make sure the proper activities are being done, tracking results and informing the Owner. The Staff will settle into the regular work.

During the Expansion element, the time for the change goes back to the different Discovery, Planning, and Implementation times. If the change is small then use a simple plan, or a bigger change add to the Master Plan, and for large changes use the HR and other plans.

There is an optional advance way to identify and clarify who does what and the amount of engagement with certain activities. When you have numerous employees, you should create a basic or comprehensive Roles and Responsibility matrix (RACI). This is a table with the rows representing roles or activities. The columns represent a person or position. One of four values can be entered or it is blank if the person is not involved with that activity.

Here is a brief explanation.
- Put an "R" in the cell if the person is **Responsible** for the activity. They do most of the work.
- Put an "A" in the cell if the person is **Accountable**. They are the "throat to choke" if

something goes wrong. Every activity must have "one" Accountable person. It is possible this person is also a Responsible.

- Put a "C" if they are **Consulted**. They are actively involved but not responsible.
- Put an "I" if they are **Informed**. They are told what is going on, but do not provide input (unless something very unusual is happening).

RACI Matrix

	John - Mrktg	Sue - Acctg	Dale - Ops	Dawe - IT
Activity 1	A	C	I	
Activity 2	I	A,R		
Activity 3	C		A	
Activity 4		C	A	R

The amount of HR work will vary depending on the business entity, classification and number of employees, and the complexity of the work. There is very little HR work when your income goes onto your personal income tax return. When the income is treated as a corporation or you have several employees, have a HR service company do your Payroll and all related work. You could get to a point you can afford a qualified HR person. Hiring others will save time and effort to focus on what you are responsible for as the owner.

Story:

Have you ever seen a TV show called Restaurant Impossible with Robert Irvine on the Food Network? Restaurant owners that are struggling or on the verge of failing contact the show, explain their situation, and ask for help. This is a little different topic because the business is already operating, but it is a great example of typical business issues and "genius" people learn from the mistakes of others and applying the knowledge.

On the show Robert goes to the restaurant to see the theme and design, the condition, the service level, food quality, how it is managed, and other factors. He has them prepare numerous menu items to test the service and food quality.

Obviously these restaurants are doing poorly in all or most of the majority categories, or they would not be on the verge of failing. There are other reasons for struggling such as their passion decline, the employees and owners are burned-out, and the owners, managers and staff are dysfunctional.

Robert is a chef and owns successful restaurants so he knows what needs to be done. He goes through all the aspects of their business to find the issues. He has a tough love approach which creates conflicts with most of the owners, managers, and staff. His intent is fix everything, including relationships.

One of his solutions is making sure that the roles are defined and who is responsible for what job. If someone does not fit, they find another position, or they leave. He gets the owners thinking and working on owner responsibilities. He gets the managers working on their responsibilities. He gets the staff working on their responsibilities.

Beyond the HR work, he spends up to $10K to renovate the restaurant. He also makes sure the other business aspects are functioning properly by revising the menu, shows how to prepare fresh and tasty food, improves the service level, understanding the business costs to determine how much to charge, and other issues.

The primary point of the story is to understand there is an owner, manager, and staff position level. You and the people you hire need to spend time in your respective role. As you think and act as the owner, try to be objective and be aware of issues. Listen to constructive feedback. Get periodic assistance from experts who are experienced and can provide a fresh view, accept and implement good ideas to stay on track.

Tip:

Do some research on the Ritz Carlton about their hiring and training process. Read about Zappos online shoe company for mission and values. Read about other companies you can think of for great ideas.

When interviewing people share the business's vision, mission, and talk about the culture and expectations. Employees who understand and follow these are an extremely important part of your success. It is best to find the right people with the proper mindset for the job. It is less about their skills because your training with develop them to your expectations. Training the skills can be far easier than training people to care about what they do.

Create a culture of trust and respect for all employees and for customers. Trust can take months or maybe years to build and can be lost in a moment if you fail them. With the training and expectations, empower employees to work together to perform the work, to solve problems and make improvements.

Chapter 7 Notes

Ideas:

Questions:

ACTIONS:

Facility and Location

66 "The great thing in the world is not so much where we stand, as in what direction we are moving." Oliver Wendell Holmes Sr. (Physician and Writer)

Your product, service, and information are major factors to determine what type of facility you need. Your type of building, customers' location, and zoning or deed restrictions will guide you to where you are located. You may or may not have the ability to decide if you rent or buy the structure. These need to be included in the funding requirements, can change over time, and are considered in your expansion plan.

This book uses facility as a general term for your house, work mobile (meet someplace), office building, retail, warehouse, shop, or other type of structure.

You should begin your business journey from your house. Many people start operating their business in a house, garage or apartment. It can be smaller products, services or information. Well-known companies that started in a garage include Amazon, Apple, Disney, Google, Harley Davidson, Hewlett Packard, Mattel, and Maglite. Not to say you want a multi-billion dollar business.

There can be regulations that prevent you from using your house due to zoning or deed restrictions. Some cities and counties require that food products to be prepared in a permitted commercial kitchen that has certified staff. There could be other government regulations relating to the types of business that you can operate in a house.

You may be able to operate a business in your house within zoning or deed restrictions if customers and traffic are not coming and going all day or night, there are no parking issues, and you keep under the radar. The easiest businesses to operate from a house are those that sell small, low volume products, services where you leave to meet people at their business or other place, and for providing information via the internet.

A true product may be okay if small size and low volume so you are not noticed. I saw a garage that had a 6 inch slab with an industrial mill, lathe, and other machine shop equipment inside a subdivision with deed restrictions. I'm surprised he was not forced to stop.

Mobile facility refers to using your vehicle or other transportation to provide your product or services. If you are a mobile notary then your car is a facility. My SUV has a 1,500 watt inverter so I can plug my 120VAC laptop (when battery is dead) and a 4-in-1 printer, scanner, copier, and fax so I have a mini office in my vehicle. This comes in very handy when doing various types of real estate work at someone's house or other location.

Your mobile meetings could be at their house, office, or many people meet at public places like coffee houses, bookstores, fast food restaurants, and other places. At some of these locations, it is not their business to provide you with a place to do business so buy something, keep it fairly short and avoid peak times. When you are using a waitress's table and considering they work for tips, give them what you would normally tip for a meal even when you order nothing or a drink.

Some of these places have free wi-fi so you can use your laptop to access the Internet to do some work. There are other places like libraries, courts, government buildings where you can use free wi-fi. Be cautious about accessing websites that use password in the very slight chance someone is capturing your information.

You may now or in the future not want people meeting at your house or a public place so you need another place. If you need an office building there are a couple options. One option is to rent a part time or full time office from the building management. They may have additional services. Another option is to rent a part time or full time office from an "executive suite and secretarial" company. They lease a large amount of space in the building and sub-lease the offices to a business, and they usually provide other services such as a conference room you can rent by the hour or day, copier, fax, mail service, and internet access.

You could find a free standing office building that was designed as a commercial building or it was a house that was converted to an office. My primary title company has a mixture of facilities renting space in a multi-story office building, in a converted house, and in a former bank.

A retail building can be free standing, in a strip center, or mall. This would include product or certain services. You rent most of these. You may be able to buy a free standing building and rent out the space you do not need at this time. Maybe you need the space in the future as part of your expansion. Hire a management company to lease the other space so you focus on your responsibilities. Owning a mall is probably beyond your financial resources and managing it.

The amount of space required can vary from a single office to tens of thousands of square feet for a small business. There are pros and cons to each of these depending on your business and where it is located so beyond the scope of this book.

A warehouse is needed when you need to store raw materials and components to make your product, and then store the final product until shipping to a customer. The warehouse usually includes an office area. These can be free standing, part of a complex, or some storage businesses also have a warehouse and office section.

A shop is similar to a warehouse with an office. These are usually designed and built-out for a specific purpose. Most of these are free standing or part of a small strip center. An auto mechanic has multiple bays with high ceilings and doors, in ground or floor mounted hydraulic lifts, and other equipment.

You will need to decide if you rent or buy the type of facility you need now and in the near future. You may be forced to rent because there is no land or building available or it is way too expensive for you to buy.

Renting commercial space is very different than renting a house. The commercial lease is typically 3 to 5 years long and the landlord will probably want a personal guarantee so you are responsible for the rent until the lease ends, or the landlord may let you out of the lease when they find another tenant. Try to have clauses in the lease to let you out.

You should use one business entity to own the structure and another entity to operate the business to protect assets.

You may have a "triple net" lease where you not only pay the rent, you pay your portion of the taxes and insurance, maintenance, and utilities. The landlord should provide an estimate and you may negotiate a cap on these expenses. They may not have an estimate if the building is less than a year old or if the current owner does not have a record of the previous expenses.

Many office buildings require you to move in or out before or after normal business hours to avoid liabilities and interference with other tenants and visitors. Your mover may be required to cover the floor and elevator with mats to protect them. All of this adds costs and inconvenience.

Besides your house, the physical location may involve zoning and deed restrictions, be in a convenient location for your customers, be in a prestigious location for a professional appearance, and what you can afford.

If the majority of your customers are located in a certain area, then it makes sense for you to be in the same area. If you have an upscale child day care then you should be near or have easy access to a higher income residential area. I know a mobile X-ray business that covers 3 local counties so they go to the customers.

Some people want to project a certain image with their location. The saying about having one chance to make a great first impression can apply. If you customer sees your office in a class C or D building they may not be impressed and not do business with you. If you are in a high class B or A building they may be impressed. Your dilemma is that the higher class building is going to cost you a lot more for the same amount of space. Your Financial Plan needs to factor in the cost to rent or buy.

Consider starting your business from home to save money for other expenses. Consider what type of structure, where will it can or needs to be, and do you begin renting and expand later by buying something better.

Story:

I investigated doing residential care using my rental properties. This is a real estate niche for another tool in my toolbox. This would be an alternative to renting one structure to one family and rent the rooms to individuals needing personal care. I would hire a company or Director to manage the operations.

Maybe you are interested in starting an assisted living business. There are state and local regulations concerning the facility.

Assisted living can be done in a commercial structure or a house. Every state has some common and different facility requirements involving size of rooms, number of bathrooms, smoke and fire controls, disability access to all the areas, and numerous others. A challenge when buying an existing house is all the work and cost to make it compliant, and the limitation on the number of residents. You can use or build a house for 4 to 8 residents, but a commercial structure could have 200 residents.

The location of a commercial structure involves a zoned area or does not fall within a deed restriction area. If your desired location is not zoned how you need, you can request and go through a variance process to maybe get approval.

In the Houston Texas area, there is extremely little "zoning" regulations and the residential subdivisions may, or may not, have deed restrictions which control things like not operating a business or having unrelated people renting a house. There is a US Federal law that could override zoning and deed restrictions to have in a restricted location.

What type of facility do you need to start and do you have a plan to expand into something else? Can you buy or do you need to rent?

Tip:

If you have control of your facility design, consider your exit strategy. Could other businesses use the building and layout as is, or with minor or major changes? Not to say that you are going to fail, but you need to have an exit strategy before you start the business.

It could be easy for an attorney to take over the same layout as a CPA, but may want to change for their style and a small change in the number of employees. It could be difficult to use the same attorney location as a warehouse business unless they have small items that can be stored in the various rooms and use the largest room for building them.

Many businesses need certain features and functions in their building. Do people drive up, in or through the building? Is there a requirement for parking spaces? What types and size of rooms or space are needed for the reception area, office / "cube farm", operations, conference room, examination, restrooms, and others? What and where are the electrical, plumbing, and mechanical requirements?

The interior rooms could be part of the structural support which could limit or prevent another business from efficiently using this building. A possible solution for more flexibility is to build a self-supporting structure and the rooms are built within the structure. They are not used for structural support so another business could renovate the space by removing and rebuilding the walls easily and at far less cost.

Today the exterior of the self-supporting structures can look very nice with stone, brick, or wood around part or all of the building instead of plain looking steel panels.

Chapter 8 Notes

Ideas:

Questions:

ACTIONS:

Operations, Purchase, and Logistics

"**N**othing shapes our journey through life so much as the questions we ask." Gregg Levoy (Author and Lecturer)

We discussed what you provide to your customers as true products, services and/or information. As mentioned in the Product chapter, I use "product" to represent whatever you provide to your customer.

This chapter involves how you create and deliver them. How simple or complex these are depends on your business.

For this book I'll simply define components as products used in building a final product or integrated with other true products. The component products include raw material such as a steel bar, or parts such as capacitor or a circuit board, or a true product such as a motor integrated with a conveyor line.

Operation equipment and supplies are the support items to create the product. These are not sold.

This book will use a basic definition of several words. A system is a group of related processes working together as a whole. A process is a sequence of events to accomplish a specific activity. Technology is some type of device and/or software to perform an activity. These are discussed more in the next chapter.

The Operations function is about how to create the true product, service and information. A true product will probably require some form of production to build it. A service will require acquiring the knowledge and skills to perform the service. Information is your knowledge and requires gaining it, organizing it into a meaningful source, and being able to communicate it.

The purchasing involves buying items directly involved in creating what you provide such as components. There are operations supporting items like production equipment and supplies. There are general business items like office equipment and supplies.

Logistics is about getting everything you need into and through the facility, and then delivering the final product to the customer.

True Products:

A true product can be made by you, your staff, or by another company as outsource. At this point you have decided on the type of facility and location to start the business. This can change later.

Creating your true product will require equipment and tools, components and supplies, and the processes. This does not need to be complex and may be fairly inexpensive to set up. If you want a bigger and more complex business now or later, then you have more work to do and it could cost tens of thousands or a million dollars to set up.

If you have a basic product that needs minimal work then you and a few people could do the work. However, remember your role as the owner and manager so you cannot spend all your time on making the product. You need your operations to quickly get to the point of having staff and technology do this work.

When your business is not able to build all of the components of the product, you can outsource it to a company that will build your component(s) or even the final product. There a various names with some differences, so I'll use Original Equipment Manufacturer (OEM). An OEM may have its own product line and decides to build for other companies. They have certain capabilities, economies of scale to buy supplies and components cheaper than you can, and have additional capacity to make it. You will not need to spend millions of dollars to build this facility, have the staff to perform all the work, and you can focus on other business functions.

Your clothing and alteration business is fairly simple – not to say it does not take knowledge and skills. Some tools include scissors and tape measure. The major equipment is a sewing machine and an adjustable mannequin. The components include the fabrics, and buttons or zipper. The supplies include thread, pins, removable chalk. The process to make the clothing is the sequence that involves cutting, sewing, fitting, and adjusting to create that garment.

The system and processes includes the patterns and using the mannequin. The technology involves the sewing machine to do embroidery. Your knowledge and skills is the ability to use all of this to make some type of clothing.

Your motorcycle business could be fairly simple. You buy the major components and outsourcing all the major work. Your work is some customization and the final assembly. The core of your business is the marketing and networking to find customers and add the final touches.

Your motorcycle business could be a full function shop. You have numerous common and specialized tools.

The equipment includes mills, lathes, high power electric hammers, bending machines, and others. The systems include powerful computers with computer aided design software that controls some of the equipment, and others. The technology can allow unusual designs and materials to add the WOW.

The components include raw materials like sheet metal and metal tubing, basic components like the head and tail lights, etc. The supplies include welding clamps, grinding wheels, and build a jig. The process is the sequence of taking everything and assembling it, painting and polishing, testing, and making any adjustments. The technology can include faster, easier, and more efficient ways to do the work. This full shop can be expensive to set up and will required skilled staff.

Your product will involve ordering, payment, packaging, and delivery. How customers order relates to the type of business and products, and where you are located. This can include a smart phone app, a computer system at your location, filling out a physical or online form, and others. Who enters the order includes you, your staff, the customer online, or a customer service company.

There are different ways to get paid. The when includes in advance, at the time of sale, or later from an invoice. The how includes cash, physical or electronic check, a merchant and gateway account for debit or credit cards, or an integrated online system.

The packaging and delivery will vary. The packaging will vary from no packaging to crating it. The type of packaging will depend on the size, shape, and how fragile it is. This includes a bubble envelop, cushioning in a cardboard box, strapped down or a custom crate. The delivery includes pickup, postal system, private common (FedEx, UPS), or a commercial carrier (hot shot, semi truck).

With the motorcycle the customer can just ride off into the sunset, or it can be loaded on a trailer or put in a crate for delivery. The garment might be handed to the customer with or without a generic or custom bag.

A true product can be built by you or your staff, outsourced to another company, or a combination. Typically there will be some type of operations performed to make the final true product, unless you are a distributor reselling an existing product. The majority of products will require purchasing something to make the final product. There will be type of logistics to bring what is needed, move to various places within the business, and the shipment.

Services:

Many of the services relate to knowledge and skill such as plumber, attorney, consultants, maid, and numerous others.

For services your core business does not providing a true product. You will probably need some true products as tools and equipment, some supplies, and processes. These may be very cheap or fairly expensive.

Your maid business's service is to clean the house. You purchase products and supplies to use. Some products include a vacuum cleaner, broom, sponges, and others. The supplies include multiple types of cleaners, cleaning towels, and others.

Your operations involve processes about how to clean certain things, what gets cleaned before something else (clean ceiling fans before vacuum floor), and maybe a system for scheduling and accounting.

Your facility can be your house or maybe an office or warehouse. Your logistics will involve going to the store to purchase what you need. The delivery is you going to the customer's house.

There is a wide variety of consulting type work. Your consulting business could involve a certain industry and/or business function such as oil and gas project manager, financial planning, or welding inspection. The operations, purchasing, and logistics will vary depending on the type of work and customer requirement.

A consulting business core business does not have a true product to build or ship. The primary operation is what you know. You are hired to provide information which can include writing reports, making presentations, and maybe do the work of an employee such as entering data into a computer or "rolling up your sleeve" to weld a part. You could have a true product as supporting materials such as selling class binders and workbooks, and CD/DVDs.

You will purchase general office equipment and supplies. You would need to outsource or purchase materials to create the binders and workbooks, and CD/DVDs as part of your true product, and may have special tools or equipment to perform the work.

Your logistics could as simples as walking from the kitchen to your home office, commuting to your office, or commuting to the customer's location. True product delivery could be bringing them with you or shipping to the location.

Logistics could include flying that requires purchasing the airline tickets, transportation and parking, hotel, meals, and other activities. You could spend additional money on entertaining customers.

Service businesses can have a fairly basic website for marketing awareness, information about you, and add credibility. You could have a method for customers to buy products you sell. There is more information about websites in the Information section below.

Certain businesses can operate without a website. Customers find them through non-online advertising, referrals, and networking. Orders can be done at a location, phone, or email. Invoicing can be done at the location, mailed, or email. The payment can be made at the location, mailed, or online service like PayPal or merchant account.

You will need services for work you cannot or do not want to perform, or not worth your time. You need to decide what services you need to start and operate your business and then find someone to provide it.

Your business could provide knowledge and skills to perform work for your customer. You may provide a true product to support what you do.

Information:

In this section, your business is to gather and make your information available to multiple people and/or companies. It is a separate section because there are so many businesses providing information only. They do not have any true products and they do not provide a service. However, some information products relate to a true product or service.

One type of information product involves a company needing to know what is happening inside and/or outside of the company. A company can gather internal data and transform it into usable information to make various decisions. This company also needs information from outside the company to be combined with their internal information for the same or other decisions.

Your business could provide the outside information. The information can relate to one or more business functions. Most external information relates to marketing, competitive review, operational, and economic.

I'll use three categories of information. They are information specifically requested by the company, information about your industry or business, and general information.

A company wants some specific information to make a decision about a new advertising campaign. The company has a target customer and needs to create an email list to send the message. Your company has a blog with thousands of people similar to this target. You sell the information to the company and deliver it electronically.

There can be an overlap between information and services products. If you help them determine the target customer, you are acting as a consultant.

Another company wants some information to expand into another city. Your business is a trade organization that represents this industry that companies subscribe to. You become the authority that people rely on. You sell certain information about businesses in that city. The company will use this to decide if they want to move into this city, where to locate, what they provide, and other decisions.

Another company is struggling and wants to find out why so they can decide what to change. Your business collects and has access to local economic information. You sell them the economic information and the company integrates with their internal information. Their analysis identifies some issues they can work to correct.

The true product can be raw data or consolidated into information. It can be delivered through online access, an integrated data feed, a published report, or verbal or written presentation.

A second type of information product has become very common and growing rapidly. It is not used for making business decisions like the first type. Your information is used by a person or company to accomplish an objective.

There are a massive number of topics with some being broad and some being a narrow niche. Some broad examples are how to do start a business, invest in real estate, improve your health, train your animal, and hundreds of others. A niche for these would be how to start a Chiropractor business, wholesale strip centers, an Army style boot camp workout, and a Labrador duck hunting retriever.

The majority of this information is a digital product because it is provided on a website and/or using various types of files. There can be an overlap between an information product and a true product. An example is providing DVD videos on your website. It is digital information you are selling separately on a physical disk. These true products become an additional revenue source. I would not classify an instructional DVD you provide free relating to specific product as an overlap. It is part of a true product.

For example a fisherman buys a rod and reel and gets a free video on how to assemble it and add the line. This is part of the true product. The video would be a true product if it is sold separately on a DVD.

You need to provide a high amount of value to really help people accomplish their objective. It is also to build credibility and trust for a long term relationship. As discussed before, be leery of information with "Get Rich

Quick", or the "7 Secrets to ___", and other marketing clichés. This can have a little legitimate information, be useless in accomplishing your objective, and/or be a scam.

With your information product, you may need to purchase access to raw data and other information. You review, analyze, and process everything so it becomes your product. You may need to pay a person or company to do this for you.

Items to purchase include equipment, software, and supplies. The equipment can be as simple as a basic computer, monitor and a multiple purpose printer, or maybe expensive high performance computers, network system and dedicated internet line. The simple software are word processing, spreadsheet, and presentation, or maybe expensive for doing business analysis and projections. The simple supplies are paper and ink, or maybe expensive presentation materials.

Once you create the information content, the files can be stored on your computer to provide the information or the files can be uploaded to a server that your website can provide. If you have very large files, there are other companies that store and provide the files faster. For information products delivered digitally you really must have a website.

Technically you could deliver small information files by sending an email. The manual work to manage emails can become overwhelming quickly. You cannot provide multiple pages of information in an email. The email does not have a way to control access to paid files so someone could forward your premium paid information to hundreds of people.

Do not use Gmail, Yahoo, or other free services to send the same message to many people on a regular basis. The current email spam detection systems will send these messages to the "spam" folder which really hurts your business – people do not get the information they requested or paid for.

Use a reputable email service company integrated into your website to register and maintain the customer information. The email service business uses your domain related email address such as yourname@yourcompany. com. The company has certain processes and requirements that flag the emails as compliant with internet spam protocols so they have an extremely high probability of going to the person's "inbox".

The bottom line – if you provide information through the internet, get a proper website. The website needs to be integrated with a proper email service company that uses a process for extremely high email delivery rates.

There are several options for creating your website. There are companies that can create your entire custom website with all the related functions. There are companies that provide industry related templates with all the website functions that are relatively easy for you or someone to modify. You may be able to create a basic website by getting a domain, setting up hosting, using WordPress template with a theme with some plugins to setup integration with an email service, ordering and payment system(s), and you or someone creates the page content.

Regardless of who creates a functioning website, the content is extremely important.

How elaborate your website is depends on the type of product(s) and the image that represents you and the business.

The website appearance can be serious or funny, a passive or aggressive message, a conservative or dynamic layout, and should include pictures and videos. Some of the pages can only be accessed through a membership or paid system.

A website can be very basic. The website has some information about you and/or business. It should allow people to register so you can occasionally send them information to maintain a relationship. There may not be anything to sell on your website.

Your maid or plumbing company can have information on 1 or 2 pages to show case you, but nothing to sell. A small bakery could have a similar type of website, but add the ability for customers to order items for pickup, delivery or shipment. Many people use PayPal as a simple way to store products for sale, create an order, provide online order information to print the list of products purchased and the delivery information, and get paid.

Your more comprehensive business needs other systems that are all integrated with the website. Some systems include customer record and communication, product creation and storage, order management with shopping cart, payment processing, and product delivery.

Do not get overwhelmed with this. Today's technology can create the website and integrate all the systems fairly easy, or better, hire someone.

Depending on which website technology, a common way systems are integrated is with Application Programming Interface (API). This is something you can be aware of, but DO NOT need to know how to create. For example, the customer registration process creates the customer record and automatically enters them into your email service company system. Your order system automatically sends the information to the payment system, then to the operations system to deliver it, and to the email service company to send the receipt.

With this technology, it is easier for other people to create your website with the proper functions so it is cheaper. Use some of the information you have gathered so a website developer can understand how to structure the website and others can create the content.

It does not matter which type of product you provide to meet your customers' needs, so I'll let you decide if it is a true product, service, and/or information product. Your business's product is to meet or exceed your customers' expectation or accomplish their objective.

Story:

We are bombarded with information every day. I read a science article in a newspaper that says we are exposed to the equivalent of 174 newspapers every day. This is not to say we read this much, but it includes everything we see and hear. My point is we have a bunch of information going into us.

Some information that is important or critical to you, has no value or relevance to someone else. The vast majority of information has nothing to do with you such as listening to the traffic report on roads that you do not use, something happens to someone you do not know, something happens in another city or country that you have no association with, advertising something with no relevance or interest to you, and other useless junk.

There is some information that may peak your curiosity for several seconds or days and then it fades away.

A sliver of information sinks in and you remember it. It aligns or conflicts with something you already know. It can fit a current want or need, or you recall it in the future. Better yet - you do something about it.

I saw a State Farm advertisement – the French Model commercial was amusing the first couple times I saw it. It is about a man saying he is documenting his accident on his phone "app". She said she did not think they had an app for that. He asks where she heard that and her answer was on the Internet. He asked if she believe that and her answer was yes. Their conversation goes back and forth about if the information on the Internet is true. She says everything on the Internet is true. She needs to leave because her online French model date is coming. It is obvious he is not a French person based on how he pronounced "bonjour". It is unlikely he is a "model".

In trying to decide if the information is wrong or great, consider who is writing the information. Do more research.

Also be cautious of reviews, particular now with all the online methods. Many are legitimate with both good and bad comments. However, there are people who provide inaccurate good and bad reviews.

I know someone who was severely criticized in several online places and they tracked the IP address back to a competitor who had never bought the information. There are probably employees and friends of owners who post great reviews that are not accurate.

The point is you cannot always believe everything you hear, read, or see. On a 20/20 TV show they showed marketing brochures of hotels and tourist locations that had major photo manipulation to embellish or out-right lie about the place. A hotel in Europe showed a blue sky, but the real picture had a nuclear power plant behind it.

It can be tough sometimes to know what is great, good and bad information. Think about who and where you get the information from. Do they have an "agenda" to steer you to their opinion and maybe take action that is not in your best interest? Is there steering being done with honest intentions?. Look for more information if it does not seem right or is an outrageous statement. Talk with other people that "know" about this – some people may hear or see the same false information. Proceed with caution and be prepared to make a change if unsure.

Tip:

Set up time slots for specific types of work. It does not matter if you have one or many roles in the business, you will have lots of work to do. It is very easy to get focused or consumed by some work and forget or ignore other important or critical work.

People with a JOB have meetings booked for various purposes. So you need to be smart and more efficient so you create and follow a weekly schedule of activity slots that includes certain types of work that you need to do.

There is lots of research about your daily physical and mental cycles, and there are numerous factors that affect these. It is beyond the scope of this tip to dispute or verify this. You should be aware of how physically and mentally sharp or zombie like you are at various times of the day. Over a week or two you might get an idea of your higher and lower times during the day. Plan thinking type activities when you are mentally sharp – for me it is in the morning. Plan physical type activities when you are get sleepy – mid afternoon.

Build it some breaks particularly when you sit or stand for long periods of time, doing the same work like using a computer or repetitive work. Also when you are low mentally and physically, take 5 or 10 minutes to walk around (go the restroom – an ironic word when you are tired), drink some cold water, talk briefly with someone, or other physical activity.

Chapter 9 Notes

Ideas:

Questions:

ACTIONS:

Systems, Processes and Technology

" T he real mark of the creative person is that the unforeseen problem is a joy and not a curse." Norman H. Mackworth (Psychologist and Scientist)

The systems and processes are created to operate the business and some of these involve technology. These involve all the business functions and aspects of your business to various degrees.

There are various definitions for system, process, and technology. Some of the definitions are vague so here are the basic definitions for this book and for you to use.

A system is a group of related processes working together as a whole. It is a high level identification. There are no specific activities or tasks to perform. Some examples are ordering system, filing system, and production system.

A process is a sequence of events to accomplish a specific objective. The process usually has an input, action, and output. There are usually other processes before and after a process. Some examples are customer entry process, payment process, and product manufacture process.

Another term to mention is procedures. A procedure steps through all the activities to perform a task. The majority of the procedures involve documents with text, diagrams, and flowcharts.

The procedures are used to do proactive training of new employees and reference information for existing employees. I worked for a company that required everyone a couple times a year to go through an online training session with questions that needed a response to verify that we understood the information.

For example your high volume costume jewelry business has an ordering system involving a true product you assemble and ship to a customer.

The ordering system will involve information from the Customer Service, Logistics, and Finance business functions.

The system will include several processes. Some of the processes include find or create the customer record, inventory available, invoice, payment, package, and ship.

Each of the processes will have a set of procedures. A basic payment procedure will use the customer's contact and credit card number information, verify the credit card, transfer money to your bank account, confirm the payment, send a receipt, and create an inventory ticket to pull the items.

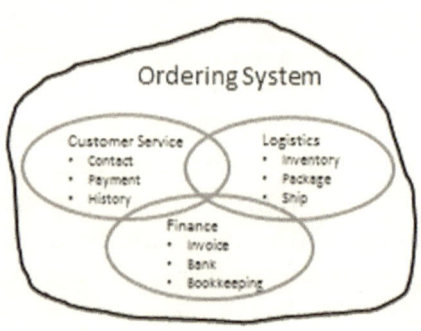

Technology is some type of device and/or software to perform an activity – yes, a very general statement. The device may require a person or some type of an interface to operate it, and it can be partially or fully automated.

An example is a computer. A person will manually use the keyboard and mouse. It has software to perform an activity such as creating a text document. For automation, the word processing software has a spell checker which automatically corrects some misspelled words, or it is partially automated when it displays several possible correctly spelled words for you to pick, or it does not know the word and you teach it by manually adding it to the dictionary.

The computer could be operated with an interface such as a bar code scanner. Depending on the process, there may or may not be any activities for a person to do. In a retail store, the scanner automatically initiates and complete the sales transaction and the employee manually hands the receipt and package to the customer. In a warehouse, the scan process could automatically retrieve an item from a storage location, and deliver it via conveyors to the back of a truck with no person involved.

Side note about systems, processes, and technology – I realized the trend for companies to reduce their customer service when gas stations stopped pumping gas, washing your window and checking the oil. Now we have self-serve stations – although a couple US states prohibit self-serve gas stations. They have systems and processes with technology for the customer to act like an employee.

The self-service function with systems, processes, and technology are going into other industries like large grocery stores. Do you use the self-check by scanning and bagging the items, and using a machine for the payment? I typically do because it is faster.

There are controls to help prevent theft and the sale of restricted items. There is a package area weight scale where you place the item in a bag and the system verifies what you scan is what you bag, and stop the checkout when a restricted item is scanned such as alcohol and the attendant overrides the stop. There are security cameras, exit door sensors, and other controls.

There are advances in technology to make it easier and faster for self-serve customers. There are companies now using and improving Radio Frequency Identification (RFID) technology to identify you and the items. You may have RFID and not realize it. Do you have a small plastic card on your key ring to tap on a credit card device, or a tag on your car windscreen for toll booths?

When you go to your grocery store in the near future, you just put the items in the cart and walk out the door without stopping. The RFID knows who you are, what is in your cart, how to pay for it, processes the transaction, and emails you the receipt. If any information is missing, an alarm goes off.

Why do some business struggle or fail? Not creating and using appropriate systems, processes, procedures and utilizing available technology are common reasons. Creating these will help eliminate gaps, allow employees to do their work more efficiently, and/or have fewer employees.

The more you can systemize, consolidate, and automate, the less manual work that needs to be done. The work could be done easier, faster, and more accurately. These will reduce expenses when done properly. The intent is to simplify, but unfortunately sometimes people do not investigate, test, or plan properly so the processes and/or technology creates complexity and inefficiency. Be smart about how you want to operate the business and keep as integrated as possible.

Story:

Ray Kroc bought McDonalds from the McDonalds brothers not to sell hamburgers, but to build a business to sell franchise opportunities to other people. He knew to create systems and processes to the degree that an owner did not need to be a restaurant expert or even have a lot of business knowledge to be successful. Owners and managers attend MacDonald's Hamburger University to learn how to operate the business. Look at the 20 to 30 year olds managing a multi-million dollar operation.

McDonalds has been very innovative in all aspects of the business and they use technology as much as possible. Every piece of equipment has a purpose(s), it is designed to be efficient, it ties into systems, processes, and there are detailed procedures. McDonalds is always looking for better ways to do everything. They will take ideas and study them, determine what changes are needed to existing operations, create the associated systems and processes, implement the change, and then test and measure the results.

I realize McDonalds spends millions of dollars to create and improve every aspect of the business for the owners. You must take the time, effort, and an appropriate amount of expense to make improvements and expansions for your future benefits.

With our executive business service business, we needed to change to align with some technology. There came a time no one needed the Telex machine and manual typewriter. With customers needing Internet access for their computer and fax, we invested in a phone system for them to use. The technology changes required us to change our processes and procedures. Our business, like everyone's, is to provide value to our current and future customers. You need to make appropriate changes or your customers go to a competitor who provides what they need.

Tip:

This takes the story and applies it to you. You need to spend some of your time, effort, and resources to create and improve your systems, processes, procedures and technology. Take a hint from McDonalds and just about every successful business. At your job, understand what works well and does not work well. What can apply to your business? Step back from your business to review and determine what to create and improve, and how to do it?

Try to keep these as simple as you can and still have the functionality to operate the business with minimal work. What can you improve or create?

Chapter 10 Notes

Ideas:

Questions:

ACTIONS:

Finance, Accounting, and Measurements

" **...a**sk not what your country can do for you; ask what you can do for your country ...". John F. Kennedy (former President of United States)

According the US Small Business Administration (SBA) and other sources, small businesses collectively are the largest creators of jobs in the United States. Therefore, one of the best ways to help the country is to start and operate a successful business.

All the core business functions and aspects are critical – that's why they are the core. Business finance, accounting, and measurements are no exception. I left this to the last business function because all the other functions will involve money and performance. You will use certain information you have gathered to complete the activities associated with this chapter.

A key to success is "know your numbers". Carefully manage your expenses from the very beginning of your journey. Once you start receiving revenue, continue to be frugal to have cash available for expansion and business dips. Cashflow is critical.

Finance is the control and management of assets (including cash) and liabilities. Use the information to make decisions about capital requirements, financial strategy, cashflow, and others. The goal is to forecast and evaluate the business performance, and help make corrections. Some of the key outputs are the Budget and various Ratio Reports, Risk Analysis, and Break-even Analysis.

Accounting is the gathering of appropriate data and transactions to prepare statements and reports. Use the information for analysis, record keeping, tax reporting, and other purposes. The goal is to understand how the company is performing, and where and what is involved in making improvements. Some of the key outputs are the General Ledger, Profit and Loss, Balance Sheet, and Cashflow Analysis.

For small businesses the Finance and Accounting functions are combined. As mentioned numerous times through this book, consider using your CPA or financial professional.

The Budget is the financial foundation to your business used by you, any partners and lenders, and other people helping you. It uses certain information you gather to make assumptions on expenses and sales to create estimated amounts. The budget is created shortly after you begin your journey with the startup costs.

Be honest with your evaluations. The estimates need to as accurate as possible, but they will be wrong to some degree because they are estimates. Be more conservative by reducing revenue and increasing expense estimates to see if the business is still worth doing.

At least every month compare the actual revenue and expenses to the budget. Work with a competent professional to help evaluate the results. Do NOT randomly make changes to the budget, but investigate what is causing the variation and how can you get back on track.

The Ratio Reports compare two or more values into another value. Depending on the type and size of your business, there could be 10 or 30 or more. Some common ratios include income with debt, income with assets, income with investment, assets with debt, and equity with debt.

The Risk Analysis evaluates what could happen and what could be done proactively to prevent or minimize. This can include some financial information. You will reduce your stress level knowing in advance how to respond if something happens.

The Break-even Analysis helps estimates when you will become profitable. This could be for the entire business or for a product. It is also used for a significant expansion.

The financial work for a single attorney will not need a complex Risk Analysis, but it is still a good idea to write down what could go wrong and what should be done to avoid and resolve them. For example, what happens if you get sick for a couple weeks or months, what happens if you lose a major customer, what happens if your building has damage, or your computer or network fails? This is not to sound doom and gloom, but things happen and it is better to have an idea of what to do before something happens.

The attorney should know where they are making and spending money so that they know how to maximize the business. With a simple analysis of the revenue and expenses for the different services such as Divorce, Bankruptcy, and Probate, you can know which is the best and expand it. Remember "intentional congruency"? You should continue all the services for customer support and diversification. Being involved in Trademark and Patents is not a good idea unless you hire a competent person(s) and your time is a couple hours a week.

Every company will require some form of a General Ledger to create the Profit and Loss Statement, Balance Sheet, and recommended Cash Flow Analysis. These and the majority of reports are used for business analysis and status to owners and company stakeholders (people who have an interest in what you and the business do). These analyses are to understand the business financially, compare certain time periods for trends, and make decisions to change or add something.

Saying you made $20,000 in June may be great, good, poor, or bad. You need to compare it to the previous month, quarter, and year. In June last year if you made $30,000 you are down, or if it was $10,000 you are up – year over year. Then compare to two years ago to see the trend.

Obviously when you are starting there will not be a last year and the startup costs are onetime. However, what you will compare is your budget to the actual expenses.

The Profit and Loss has the income and expenses to determine the Gross, Net, and other types of profit. Hopefully your only loss is during startup and shortly after opening. This is also needed for tax reporting.

The Balance Sheet has assets, liabilities, and equity (net worth). This is used to indicate the strength of the business. You want far more assets (value) than liabilities (owe). The remaining amount is the net worth of the business.

The Cashflow Analysis includes money coming in and going out for each month for one year and quarterly for the second and third years. Estimating the values can be challenging, but your Discovery activities will help determine the expenses, pricing, sales volume, and other information to use.

A decent size retail store needs to have far more financial information to know what and how much to buy and when. If they are very seasonal, then a Cashflow Analysis is extremely important so you can maximize sales (have proper products and quantity) in the peak times and have money available when it is slow. Most of your cash out is early summer when you are buying the majority of your inventory to arrive in October for the Christmas peak sales. Most of your revenue comes in December. Do you have enough cash to pay for everything before you can put money in the bank? Then you may have customers who are slow or do not pay you. The Cashflow Analysis will factor in the delays and a small percentage of bad receivables.

Every business needs to know its fixed and variable expenses. The fixed expenses occur even when you do not make or sell anything. This includes rent, insurance, basic utilities, equipment leases, and others. The variable expenses change when you make your product. This includes components, additional utilities, shipping, and others. Both can change as you do expansions.

If your business is fairly complex like the machine shop, then you will need to tie the financial and accounting work with the operations. It is important to combine these so that you know the product related costs to prepare custom quotes quickly and accurately. If you have standard products, you need current and accurate costs to create and revise price lists or how much you can discount.

A key aspect of financing is to make sure that you have all the funding you need to start, operate, and expand the business. Lack of funding is one of the major reasons businesses fail.

The funding can come from different sources and for different purposes. There are numerous sources for funding from your own savings (good reason to keep your present job and save more money while starting the business). You could borrow from family and friends but take extra care - consider how this could affect your relationship if it does not work and having them as a partner giving you advice.

You may be able to get some type of loan for the rest. It may be a personal or commercial loan, or a US Small Business Administration "guaranteed" loan (they do not make the loan), or other financial institutions. You will probably need to put some money down to have "skin in the game".

Be cautious when someone says you do not need a personal guarantee on a commercial loan. This book is about starting a business and you probably will not have enough experience and business finances to override the lender's need for a personal guarantee. Let's face the fact that the lender wants some assurance their money will be paid back and if the business does not have it, they will want money from you personally. If you have great experience, have a very good credit score, put some money down, and have a compelling business plan, the lender may not need a personal guarantee.

With many commercial loans, the personal guarantee is not reported to the personal credit reporting agencies – Transunion, Equifax, and Experian. This does not affect your personal credit score. However, **if you become late on your payments** they can report this to one or more of these agencies which will drop your personal credit rating, affect your debt / income ratio, and cause other problems.

Another funding source is to have an equity partner, venture capitalist, or angel investor. They provide cash and/or credit for you to get all or some of the money to start the business. They may be active or passive in the operations of the business depending on your experience and their confidence in you performing. They get a percentage of the profit. They could provide some of the money through a loan like a financial institution, but with fewer qualifications.

You may need funding to pay some or all of your living expenses while you start the business. Starting the business while you still have a job is the core to this book – Work Yourself Out of a Job. If you are unemployed or consuming your savings, this book and the process applies, but you need to accelerate your time schedule to start the business faster, and probably start it with fewer products or services – go for quality over quantity.

Regardless of the source, funding is needed to pay the expenses to start the business. You will always be trading time and money. Some activities can be free such as you finding a domain name and writing information content.

If you want to accept debit and credit card payments, will need to find a merchant account provider and a gateway company that does not charge you a set up or monthly fee, but will charge a little more when you do a transaction. There are companies that provide more functions such as storing your product and pricing, shopping cart, and redirect the customer back to your website after they pay.

You could also hire someone to do these. The questions go back to - What is the best use of your time and what are your strengths? If I hire someone to do this activity, what activities do I do? Will I be able to start the business faster to have revenue coming in?

Funding could be needed after you start operating the business. There is working capital considering the cashflow delays, doing equipment or process improvements, and expansions. Maybe purchase another company. Some of this can come from retained profits, but you do not want to deplete your cash reserves, so funding is probably needed.

Your Information business can have no or a longer payment receipt delay. The core information is available to sell when you launch the website. Customers see some information and pay online before they receive the paid information so no delay. If you offer a payment plan, it could take 60 or 90 days to get paid. If you have a monthly subscription, you get a little over the next year or more – assuming you provide value and they stay.

There is a type of measurement called metrics. A metric is a snapshot of something that can be quantified and compared to a standard or a previous amount. Some of the financial and account information, and analysis are metrics such as all the ratios and comparing annual and monthly sales, or one period's expenses to the previous similar period(s) such as month to month or year to year.

The results are reviewed and decide if or what appropriate actions are taken. The information can be presented in reports, graphs, and maybe combined into dashboards.

Metrics involve many aspects of your business. Metrics for a salesperson include the number of calls per day, how many leads converted to sales, what is the average sale amount, how many repeat customers purchased, compare the new and existing customers' sales amount, and the list goes on.

If you have any operations, you will have metrics. Some include how many are made per a time period, how many have a quality issue, production and product tolerances, how long to pull, pack and ship, and others.

The problem with some companies is that they do not have any or the proper data or information to create metrics. The other problem is the business goes crazy doing measurements and analysis which wastes time and resources, and can lead to confusion and poor decisions.

You must "know your numbers". The routine financial statements are need so you, or an expert, can understand what is happening. Learn what and how to measure the important factors for the key business aspects to manage, and control the expansion or contraction of your business.

Story:

When we bought the executive business service, the owner financed part of it, we used a little of our money, and got a loan. This is very common when buying a business.

When moving into the second location, the space needed some redesign requiring construction referred to "build out". The owner paid for the work and our rent was increased a small amount. It saved us spending a large amount of money when we moved in. If structured properly, the landlord will make a profit over time. A win-win.

The company was a C Corporation. The sale of the company was done by selling all the shares to the new owner. This is a little unusual because the new owner has the risk of potential legal issues during the time we owned the business. Most of the sales of corporations are done by selling the assets and paying for the "goodwill" and the company is closed. The new owner creates a new company and any legal issues stay with the closed entity.

The biggest reason they bought the corporation was we had just re-negotiated a good lease contract with the building. A new company would need to negotiate a new contract and very unlikely they would have received the same terms. Also, we operated the business properly and did not have any actual or pending legal issues so there was no known risk.

The real estate industry is very unique when it comes to financing. You can "leverage" the value of the property to get a loan with no or very little money out of your pocket. Try going to a stock broker to buy $80,000. worth of stock making a very nice return for the cost of one regular steak.

When someone is able to purchase, close, and repair the property below a percentage of the "after repair value", then there is no or an extremely small amount of money out of pocket. These hard money loans cost more, but it is a trade-off to be able to do the deal. Would you rather have 100% of nothing because you did not to pay extra money, or make 20, 30, or 1,000% return of your investment, but you had to pay more for the loan.

The exit strategy to get out of higher cost loan is to refinance the property if you plan to hold for a long time so you can recover the extra costs, or immediately resell it (flip).

Tip:

At night I use a micro cassette recorder beside my bed to record ideas and information. I did not like a digital recorder because the record button is too small to see and use in the dark, and it creates a new file every time so it was more difficult to extract the information.

I have done this this for over 20 years so I can keep my eyes closed to pick it up and press the record button. I open one eye to verify the red light is recording – a few times the battery was dead and it did not record.

At any time during the night I can lie on my side away from my wife and just say whatever I'm thinking. Occasionally I'll take the recorder with me when I drive and listening to a CD so I can record notes and enter into a document later.

When I'm ready to listen, I record about 10 seconds of nothing to know when I have finished the last recording session. I rewind and write the ideas and information on an action sheet or in the appropriate document. When I get to the quiet section I know that recording session is done and then rewind to start the next session.

I learned that a notepad on the night stand did not work for me. I would not turn on a light to wake my wife, so I would write over top of other writings, the pen or pencil would not write properly, and the mental and physical actions to wake enough to reach over and find the pad and pen, and do the writing would disrupt my thoughts so the micro cassette works best for me. I just say whatever comes to mind, press pause when thinking, and un-pause when ready to speak.

Chapter 11 Notes

Ideas:

Questions:

ACTIONS:

Summary

" **D** o not wait; the time will never be ''just right." Start where you stand, and work with whatever tools you may have at your command, and better tools will be found as you go along." Napoleon Hill (Author and Lecturer)

Everyone cannot be a business owner. Corporations need employees – some with tens or hundreds of thousands. The question being posed is – Do you dislike or HATE your job enough or do you have a passion to do something else – your own business?

Some journeys to business owner are easy and can be done in several months with very little money, and others take a fair amount more. You need to have a strong "why" and a passion for doing something to start a business so you are motivated to continue your journey if people do not believe in you and when things are not going according to plan.

A small percentage of people know what business they want to do. The majority of people do not know what they want to do when they think about starting a business. It is perfectly normal to not know what type of business to start in the beginning. You can find your path as you gather and understand information. Doing this while you have a job is a great advantage.

You probably have concerns or apprehension about starting a business because you do not know what is involved. You need a comprehensive and structured process with supporting documents as the roadmap for your journey. You will have challenges so the more time and effort you spend creating the roadmap, the easier it will be and the fewer problems and disruptions.

Create and share your vision, mission, and goals with people who truly support you starting your business. They will help hold your accountable. Avoid the nay-sayers.

Work with others who have the knowledge and experience so you can be "genius" and learn from what they did right and wrong so you can plan and act accordingly. Have you considered going to a Travel Agent who has been to a different country to help you plan your trip there? They have experienced the trip and should have learned about various locations so they can share them with you. But you will create your own trip.

It is too bad a single book cannot provide every detail that you need to start and operate your business. The intent of this book is to identify and highlight key business functions and aspects with activities for you to consider, investigate, and apply in creating your journey. I have included stories and tips to help relate the information to an event or situation.

This book is not to sit on a shelf in mint condition. It is intended to be like a workbook with highlighting, underlining, putting asterisks (*) by sentences, and what I love – blank pages at the end of the chapter to write Ideas,

Questions, and ACTIONS. If you need more space for writing, then immediately create your Business Information document and add more information.

I intended with this book, the additional information and documents, various types of support available, and with your time, effort, and perseverance, that you can **Work Yourself Out of a Job, and Take Control of Your Life and Reap the Rewards You Desire.**

For additional contact and journey information, go to the company website at www.LYLBusinessDevelopment.com or send us an email at start@ LYLBusinessDevelopment. com.

General Notes

Ideas:

Questions:

ACTIONS: